Measuring, Managing, and Maximizing Performance

What every manager needs to know about quality and productivity to make real improvements in performance

Measuring, Managing, and Maximizing Performance

What every manager needs to
know about quality and productivity
to make real improvements
in performance

Will Kaydos

Productivity Press
PORTLAND, OREGON

Productivity Press
P.O. Box 13390
Portland, OR 97213-0390
United States of America
Telephone: 503-235-0600
Telefax: 503-235-0909
E-mail: service@ppress.com

Book and cover design by Hannus Design Associates
Printed and bound by BookCrafters
Printed in the United States of America

We gratefully acknowledge the President and Fellows of Harvard College for their permission to reprint "Can You Analyze This Problem?" by Perrin Stryker, originally published in the May-June 1965 issue of *Harvard Business Review,* and the Goldhirsh Group, Inc. for permission to reprint a portion of "Keeping Tabs on Your Company" by Charles J. Bodenstab, originally published in the August 1989 issue of *Inc.* magazine.

Library of Congress Cataloging-in-Publication Data

Kaydos, Will.
    Measuring, managing, and maximizing performance / by Will Kaydos.
        p. cm.
    Includes bibliographical references and index.
    ISBN 0-915299-98-4
    1. Industrial productivity. 2. Quality of products. I. Title.
HD56.K39 1991
658.5—dc20   90-20805
                                                  CIP

02 01 00 99 98 97   14 13 12 11 10 9 8 7

To John, Neely, and Emily

Table of Contents

List of Illustrations

Publisher's Foreword

WE LIVE IN AN age of change. Challenges abound continuously. We must not fear the uncertainty of these challenges. To survive, we must promote innovation and creativity in every area of our enterprises. To succeed, individual corporate leaders as well as top and middle managers must become entrepreneurial and innovative. While trying to produce the highest quality goods or services at the lowest cost, we must simultaneously explore new areas of endeavor. This challenge will not end.

To keep up with today's new manufacturing and service environments, traditional management functions must change. Through QC circles, we teach statistical quality control, quality function deployment, total quality control, and other techniques. And because today people need to know more than ever, we are giving every person in the workplace greater learning opportunities regardless of job function or department.

This new outlook on work demands performance measures in every area of the company — from CEO to receptionist, from accountant to designer, from the plant floor to the marketing offices and sales room. Will Kaydos addresses these issues in this important book, *Measuring, Managing, and Maximizing Performance*. With the voice of experience and well-deserved authority, he tells us what managers need to know about quality and productivity to make real improvements in performance.

This is a straightforward accounting of today's work environment. It talks us through setting up a quality and productivity improvement program — and explains why most such programs fail. It reminds us of the often forgotten basic principles underlying a successful improvement program: commitment, willingness to change, the ability to listen, and a balance of ambition and patience. And that is just Chapter 1.

The body of this extraordinarily well-written book is a thoughtful narrative on performance measurement and performance management. After calling our attention to the fact that all productivity problems are ultimately caused by poor quality (Chapter 2), it discusses the most valuable benefit of proper performance measurement — a sound understanding of how the production system works and the forces that drive it (Chapter 3). A discussion follows on key performance factors (Chapter 4) and measuring the performance of a production process. Here, the author's emphasis is on information — that the quality of any decision is limited by the information available when it is made. Managers at every level need performance information at the actionable level — and it is often missing. This results in managers who are blissfully unaware of many problems to be solved and potential opportunities. It is obvious today that traditional accounting systems alone cannot fill all of management's information needs for effective decision-making. They must be supplemented by systems that measure operational performance (Chapter 5). And this brings the author around to Statistical Process Control, which he insists should not be a black art that frightens managers. In Chapter 6, entitled "The Simple Truth about Statistical

Quality Control," he reminds us that measuring performance is only the first step to improving performance. Also, while some processes are complicated and may demand sophisticated statistical techniques, most quality problems are not complex and require only simple graphs or run charts.

Chapter 7 goes into the right way to solve problems, urging managers to utilize cross-functional teams and to expand the boundaries of the problem — two effective ways to overcome biases that everyone acquires over time. At this point, we are reminded that healthy profits do not mean performance cannot be improved. Successful companies and managers seek continuous improvement and the author discusses methods that can be applied in nearly any business activity to find opportunities and to estimate their potential value (Chapter 8).

Because beliefs and values affect how people see the world and react to it, Chapter 9 tackles culture. An organization's culture and accompanying social characteristics are important because they complement and maximize the technical tools and processes needed to improve quality. Indeed, the first step in improving quality is to start changing the culture. The author approaches this methodically and offers procedures to follow (Chapter 10).

Chapter 11 focuses on managing performance. It explains and narrows the gap between actual and desired performance, emphasizing the key elements of communicating and learning. Finally, the author states unconditionally that low blue-collar productivity is a result of poor white-collar performance. And that no matter what color the collar, all performance is vital to a business and must be measured. Chapter 12 looks at applications: measuring white-collar performance, measuring sales performance, service industries, applications at the department level and broader, and the limitations of measures.

Can any of us not afford to read this book? I don't think so. I have yet to find anything that gives us so concisely the essentials of performance measurement theory, a practiced set of implementation methods, and application overviews. This volume is the best of its kind in an area that is important right now. Will Kaydos has spent the past two decades implementing his ideas and methods in companies that have testified to their validity. Rave reviews are in. Take a look at the testimonials to the author's work and then read the book. You will not be sorry — in fact, I bet you will pass it on to others in your company.

This book is an addition to Productivity Press's Quality Management Series. In producing this quality book, I wish to acknowledge the people who worked together to make it so: Cheryl Rosen, series editor, who recognized the value of Will Kaydos's work and sparked all of our interest; Marie Cantlon, managing editor; Holly Miller, freelance copyeditor; Nancy Hubert, publicity manager; Kathlin Sweeney, production, who handled the endless details of our production process; Dick Hannus, jacket designer; Rudra Press for art production and book composition; and Arcata Graphics for the printing and binding.

Norman Bodek
Publisher

Preface

IMPROVING QUALITY and productivity is easier than many managers think. It is not a mysterious process that can be performed only by skilled technicians or inspirational leaders. After you cut through the jargon, the underlying principles are few and simple. These principles are not new. They have been used by successful managers for centuries and can be used by any manager today. Following these principles will always produce rewarding results. Ignoring them will minimize the chances for achieving any lasting benefits.

Although many books and articles have been written about the subject, the concepts of quality and productivity are not as well understood as they should be. Neither are all the benefits available to companies, managers, and employees that come from improving performance — when it is done the right way. This lack of understanding has three negative effects: (1) when companies and managers are not aware of the opportunities they are missing, there is no incentive to get better; (2) fear of the unknown is a strong deterrent to changing anything; and (3) many attempts to improve quality and productivity will fail to produce lasting results because of incorrect approaches to the problem.

If you want to use a process, you must first understand it. This book examines the entire process of improving performance to explain why and how the process works, not just what to do. It describes how strategy, performance measurement, problem solving, and social culture interact to determine the level of performance a company will be able to achieve and maintain.

Although much of the early discussion is about technical matters, the reader should not get the mistaken idea that people play a minor role in the process. To the contrary, most of the problem and all of the solution ultimately depends on people. Without the proper social culture within a company, the value of any technical tools is quite limited. That point will be very clear when the reader has finished the book.

Improving performance is part science, part human relations, part art, and a good deal of work. It cannot be accomplished by installing a new computer, adopting the latest management fad, or conducting a motivational campaign. Instead, it is a process of constant learning and development, with the rewards being generally proportional to the investment. As Deming preaches, real increases in performance can only come from improving the production process. That requires changing how tasks are performed, how people think, and how they act. This does not happen overnight. *Those who promise magical cures and quick success not only don't understand the problem, they are part of the problem.*

Increasing productivity and quality is not a neatly packaged problem. It is a messy, poorly defined problem with no beginning and no end. There are always so many places to start, it looks like there is no place to start. However, even though the problem is unstructured, it is possible to take a systematic and logical approach to its solution.

The straightforward procedures given in this book can be used by any manager to increase the total performance of his department, division, or company. They apply equally well to both line and staff functions in any industry. Using them, results similar to those illustrated below are well within the grasp of any manager.

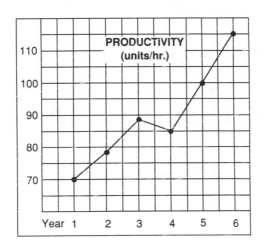

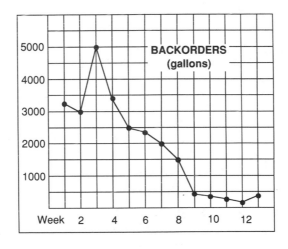

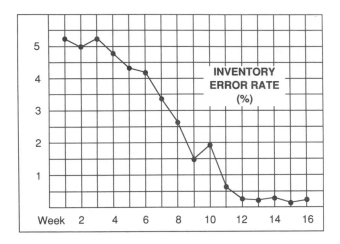

Who Should Read This Book

This book is written for every manager who could benefit from a sound understanding of how to improve performance and practical methods and procedures for getting started doing it. This applies to both administrative and manufacturing managers, from CEOs to department heads and supervisors. The concepts of quality and productivity apply to every business activity, not just to manufacturing. Indeed, as will be discussed, white-collar productivity is probably a more important issue than blue-collar productivity for most businesses.

Any manager can understand this book because it uses plain language and doesn't try to dazzle the reader with acronyms, buzzwords, and technical jargon. But that doesn't mean the problem of improving performance is trivialized. Instead, the coverage of the key issues is quite thorough. The messages in this book are important for any manager. Improving quality and productivity should be a total company effort, but individual managers can use the knowledge contained here on his or her own to improve the performance of their departments, make their jobs easier, and be recognized for their accomplishments.

Since much of the discussion is about effective use of information for making decisions, managers in information and accounting disciplines will also find this book helpful, since it will give them a new perspective on the information necessary to properly manage and control a company's operations.

Benefits

The person reading this book will come away with:

- A new perspective on quality and productivity and what those terms mean for his areas of responsibility.
- A complete picture of the basic principles that must be followed to achieve and maintain a high level of performance — what they are, why they work, and how to use them.
- New insight into how to measure performance and why performance measurement is essential for performance management.
- Practical methods and procedures that can be used to find previously hidden opportunities for improving quality and productivity.
- A specific plan which can be used as a framework for getting started on the road to continuously improving quality and productivity.

These are all significant benefits, but perhaps the most important results of reading this book will be (1) the realization that there are many areas where quality and productivity can be improved and (2) the motivation to start doing something about it.

About the Book

In many respects, this book is another way of looking at what is called "Total Quality Control." The thoughts in it are generally consistent with what authors such as Crosby, Deming, Juran, Imai, Shingo and others have said about quality and productivity. After all, the similarities between these authorities are far larger than the differences. However, since it reflects my own thoughts, experiences, and biases, there are a few significant differences between this book and others on the subject.

First, quality and productivity are examined in broad terms and are viewed as two different dimensions of what everyone calls "performance." Therefore, the general problem is performance management and improvement. If you are going to manage performance, you must first define what it means. Then, by measuring performance and the factors that affect it, a logical approach can be taken to improving it.

Second, management is seen as a process in which performance information is used to make decisions that ultimately result in improvements to the production process. In that context, Statistical Process Control (SPC) is shown to be a special kind of performance measurement where statistical analysis is used to convert data into useful information. When viewed from this perspective, the relevance of SPC to improving quality and productivity is more readily apparent.

Finally, since this is written primarily from the practical perspective of a manager who has been in the trenches, I recommend working directly through the established organization and holding managers accountable for results. After all, that's why they are getting paid. Committees and structures such as Quality Circles can be effective supplements to the formal organization, but they must not become substitutes for management or make managers less accountable for their actions. This is apparently not in conflict with general practice, but accountability is a subject which has not received much attention in other works.

Although some discussion of basic concepts cannot be avoided, the emphasis is on practical issues and applications. Theories are worthless unless they can be translated into action. For that reason, a strong effort has been made to be concise and provide specific direction without getting into rambling discussions of all the finer points of an issue. A number of good references are given for those who want to get into more detail on selected subjects.

No doubt some people will disagree with various aspects of this book. That's OK. One thing I've learned in life is that there is always more than one way to do anything. What works for one person may not work for another.

But something else I've learned is not to argue too loudly with success.

Will Kaydos

Acknowledgments

THIS BOOK IS better than it would have been without the help of many people who took the time to read initial drafts and provide constructive criticism.

John Murphy, President of Executive Edge; Tom Gelb, VP of Continuous Improvement for Harley-Davidson; Mason Epperly, Manager of Quality Assurance for Sara Lee Knit Products; John Mariotti, President of Huffy Bicycles; and William Messner, Director, Copy Products Quality Assurance for Eastman Kodak Company deserve a special note of thanks for their time, thoughtful critiques, and contributions of material.

I would also like to thank the many other readers of preliminary drafts for their comments, helpful suggestions, and words of encouragement. My conversations with these knowledgeable and experienced individuals invariably produced thoughts which found their way into this book.

My wife Susan also deserves special recognition for tolerating my long hours on the computer as well as the many hours she has spent doing research, running errands, and proofreading the manuscript in all of its many revisions.

Finally, I would like to take this opportunity to thank Clarkson University and the Texaco company for, many years ago, making it financially possible for me to pursue a college education. Without their assistance, this book would never have been written.

A Note about Endnotes

ENDNOTES ARE provided at the end of the book. The endnotes only give credit where credit is due or refer to sources of additional information on the subject being discussed. In order to avoid interrupting the flow of the material, all relevant information is contained in the text.

In other words, you can ignore them as you read and not miss a thing.

Measuring, Managing, and Maximizing Performance

What every manager needs to know about quality and productivity to make real improvements in performance

CHAPTER 1

The Foundation for Success

W ITH ANY undertaking, there are elements which are necessary for achieving success. In the case of improving productivity and quality, the cornerstone, mortar, and bricks that make up the foundation for success are one cardinal rule, four management qualities, and eight basic principles. Leaving any of these elements out of a program to improve performance will make it a very shaky structure.

The Cornerstone

The cardinal rule of improving quality and productivity is that *permanent improvement can only come from improving the production process.* The term "production process" applies to physical processes as well as any organization producing goods or services. A salesman produces sales calls, a customer service department produces answers to inquiries, and a drill press produces holes. Every individual is a production process (or production system), taking in raw materials, converting them to some other form, and delivering them to a customer. The same is true of any department, division, or company.

Although the term "production" is usually associated with manufacturing, every administrative, staff, white-collar, or service function is also a production process. On close examination, the differences between "white-collar" and "blue-collar" activities are more rooted in cultural beliefs than they are in reality. The same is true of manufacturing and service companies. Manufacturing companies perform more service functions than they realize and service companies are more like manufacturing companies than they recognize.

What does "improve the process" mean? It means improving its inherent capabilities such as efficiency, reliability, or versatility. Does giving speeches, putting up posters, or holding contests improve the process? Not really. They may be worthwhile activities, but they don't make any fundamental difference in a production system's capabilities.

Changing methods and procedures, using better materials, increasing the reliability of equipment, and training are all examples of improving a production process. Without changing the basic activities in a production process, no lasting change in its output can be expected. That is why so many efforts to improve performance fail. Almost any situation can be temporarily improved by giving it more attention, but unless the fundamental capabilities of a production process are increased, the gains will not last.

The Mortar

The mortar needed in the foundation for improving performance consists of four qualities management must have:

- Commitment
- Willingness to change
- The ability to listen
- A balance of ambition and patience

Commitment is necessary from the very beginning. Are you really prepared to pay the short term price for long term gains? There is no growth without pain and no return without investment. If you expect something for nothing, you have been reading too many business fairy tales. Like death and taxes, there are overpowering forces that govern business as well as life. Somewhere in the heavens is written:

> *Any attempt to improve any aspect of a business*
> *will always make things worse before they get better.*

Novices and most college professors think that when you have a problem you sit down at a desk, think a little bit, and then design a solution which cures the problem. That's a nice fantasy, but when you lose your chewing gum in the chicken-yard of real life, you seldom find it on the first try.

As Murphy has decreed, if anything does work on the first attempt, it's probably an illusion. The real problems will not become apparent until the change is introduced throughout the company. This strict law of nature is particularly unforgiving when you're trying to improve quality and productivity.

Success will only come with time, persistence, and investment. To succeed in the long run, it will be necessary to put up with short term problems. A lack of determination will result in halfhearted efforts and giving up at the first signs of difficulty. If you are committed, you will persevere and succeed; if you are not, don't bother to start.

Willingness to change is a by-product of commitment. Few people like change. It disrupts normal behavior, is generally seen as a threat, involves some degree of risk, and always temporarily increases the work load. Unfortunately, as shown by Figure 1.1, if you want a different output from a production system, either the input or the internal processes must change. Companies often want to improve their performance but don't want to change anything to make it happen. As soon as someone suggests changing anything, countless objections are made until about the only thing left to change is the color of the toilet paper — and that isn't going to have much impact.

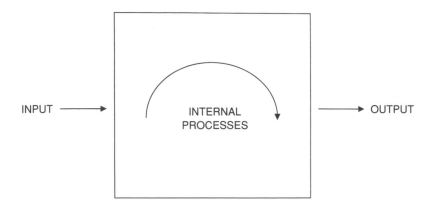

Output (0) = Input (I) Factored by Internal Processes (P)
$$\Delta 0 = (\Delta I \times P) + (\Delta P \times I)$$

If ΔI and $\Delta P = 0$, $\Delta 0 = 0$

To change the output of a production process, the input, the internal processes, or both must change.

Figure 1.1 Input/Output Relationship for any System

If you truly want to improve the performance of your business or department, you must be willing to change anything and everything. Throw out all the rules and challenge every assumption. Consider everything a variable. Tear the system apart and start over. Get someone who doesn't know "every widget maker does it that way" to review your situation.

> *Doing everything the same old way*
> *is sure to produce the same old results.*

Although everyone is a little apprehensive about changes, management's fears about upsetting the rest of the organization are totally unfounded. When management communicates properly, demonstrates commitment, and shows everyone how they will benefit, change is readily accepted. Managers are usually more cautious about making changes than the average employee, but that is probably because they are more aware of the risks and potential problems. History has shown, however, that companies which stand still are taking the highest risk of all.

A case in point is reported by Masaaki Imai who escorted Japanese businessmen visiting American companies in the 1950s. One of them, Toshiro Yamada, remarked to him that he visited the River Rouge steelworks in Dearborn, Michigan, 25 years later and that it looked exactly the same! That could never happen in Japan according to Imai.[1]

Being willing to listen and keeping an open mind about new ideas is difficult because we all have our blind spots and prejudices. It is logical to believe current practices are the best because it is true — but only until someone finds a better way. Saying something won't work and finding fault with every new idea is easy, but a manager's job is to find the one reason why something will work — not the hundred reasons why it won't.

Another important point about listening is that in most companies there is a strong tendency to discount information from the people at the bottom of the pyramid. This "not invented here" or "they don't know what they're talking about" attitude prevents many good ideas from being heard and many problems from being recognized. Admittedly, management and the technical staff are better equipped to solve some problems, but many good suggestions can come from the front line clerk, salesman, or production worker also. In any case, it is hard to argue that anyone is more aware of problems than the person who must deal with them.

If someone says he has a problem, there is no getting around the fact that the problem exists. It may be trivial to someone else, but it isn't to the person with the pain. He may be wrong about the cause of the problem and is probably reacting to symptoms, but pretending it is a figment of his imagination won't make it go away. It is a manager's job to listen, see the illness is diagnosed, and implement a cure.

While it is easy to blame hourly employees for poor performance, management decides where resources will be applied. Management also determines a company's values, objectives, strategy, and policies. That is why productivity and quality are ultimately management's responsibility.[2]

Management must listen to customers as well as to employees. Complaints and criticism aren't any fun, but they are a valuable source of information. For example, a software company was not having a great deal of success because it lacked the ability to track raw material lots through production of the end product. When this information was relayed to the President, his reply was, "I don't care what the customers are telling you, sell it to them anyway." Lots of luck.

A balance of ambition and patience is hard to achieve, but it is a practical requirement. You must reach for ambitious goals but you cannot expect to reach them overnight. Go for a 50 or 100 percent improvement, not 5 percent, but plan on it taking a few years instead of a few months. Who can get excited about improving anything by 5 percent? You probably couldn't measure it anyway.

Hewlett-Packard is a wonderful example of the value of being ambitious. In 1979, John A. Young, the CEO, challenged all division managers to improve quality tenfold within a decade. His ambitious goal required such a big leap forward, it galvanized the whole company which has made remarkable progress. "If John had asked only for an improvement of 30 percent or so, nothing probably would have been done for years," says Craig Walter, the corporate director of quality.[3]

Going after big goals will help focus everyone's attention on the long-term objective instead of on just trying to have something to show for the next quarter's report. It is worthwhile to set timetables for achieving major milestones and objectives, but it is also true that events will dictate the schedule more than vice-versa. The danger in establishing a detailed schedule is that it may become the end in itself, forcing managers to make bad decisions just to satisfy someone's prediction.

If a schedule for specific results cannot be predicted, how do you know if you're making sufficient progress? Easy. If the trend in quality and productivity is upward, no matter by how little, you're on the right track. Many bits and pieces will have to fall into place before the pace of progress accelerates. It's like tuning up an old car, it won't run well until the last bad part is replaced.

Improving productivity and quality is not a one-shot task that can be completed in a few months. It requires a change in attitude that extends from the executive suite to the shop floor. It is likely to require everyone to modify what he does and how he does it. Ocean liners cannot be turned around on a dime, but their courses can be easily changed with a little steady pressure.

The secret to many an entertainer's overnight success has been years and years of hard work. The same is true of the Japanese "miracle." Companies look at what the Japanese have accomplished and expect to duplicate their success in a year or two. They forget that it took decades for Toyota and other companies to develop their capabilities.

Progress must be made one step at a time — and making progress must never end. This requires a continuous process of problem identification, innovation, testing and implementation to take place. At first glance, making big improvements in quality and productivity may seem impossible, but it is not that difficult to accomplish when the right approach is taken. Many companies have been able to do it. Yours can too, but the path will probably be longer and the rewards greater than you think.

The Bricks

The four management qualities just described are the mortar that holds a quality and productivity improvement program together, but bricks are also needed to build a foundation. These bricks are eight fundamental principles of human behavior and problem solving that everyone "knows," but everyone forgets. Like the links of a chain, none of these principles is more important than the others, but leaving any one of them out weakens the whole structure. The bricks are:

1. *No one willingly does anything they see as not being in their own self-interest.* Why should they? You wouldn't be reading this if you didn't think you would benefit by the experience. Sometimes people seem to behave irrationally from our viewpoint, but from their viewpoint, they are completely rational. This doesn't mean we are all selfish and greedy, but none of us is going to volunteer for anything that will threaten our well-being. Minimizing pain and maximizing pleasure drives each of us according to our own personal set of values.

   Research into why supervisors frequently don't support management's decisions revealed the not-too-startling fact that they simply did not see themselves benefiting from the changes. It was usually clear to the supervisors how those below and above them would benefit, but all they could see for themselves was more work. It's no wonder they would not give enthusiastic support to new programs.[4]

   "Leadership" still lacks a commonly accepted definition, but certainly the most basic requirement of a leader is being able to convince followers that his course of action is in their interest. Gandhi and Hitler would both qualify as great leaders in this respect, even though their values were diametrically opposed.

2. *Anxiety moves people to action.* People, like rocks, don't move unless something makes them move. If there is

no difference between where people are and where they want to be, they will not change their position. Therefore, we must find a way of making them see the difference between their current level of performance and what it should be, if we want them to take action.

This doesn't mean we want to create an atmosphere where people are nail-biting nervous wrecks. The objective is to create a positive discomfort such as a goal or reward to achieve, but negative stimulation also has its place.

3. *Learning is the result of creating a stimulus, observing the response, and providing feedback to the person involved.* Without being able to associate an output to an input, learning cannot happen. Getting better at anything is a process of learning, which cannot happen without consistent feedback that links an action to a result.

   Feedback is information, so it follows that an organization's ability to improve its performance by learning depends to a great extent on the information available to its members. This means all information, not just what appears on the financial reports.

4. *There is no better way to solve problems than by using the Scientific Method.* While all the skill in the world will not beat dumb luck, it is not a very reliable way to make progress. The best way to solve a problem is to examine the facts, devise a possible solution, and then conduct an experiment to see if it solves the problem. If the proposed solution works, then the changes can be implemented across the board. If not, the cycle must be repeated, taking advantage of what was learned.

   The Scientific Method is as applicable in business as it is in the research laboratory. Businesses, however, tend to be less disciplined than laboratories. When quality or productivity problems are involved, it is easy to find people jumping to conclusions not supported by facts.

Reacting to symptoms usually leads to applying solutions to problems that don't exist.

The Scientific Method is the only logical way to solve problems. Note, however, that using it requires the ability to observe or measure how something is behaving before, during, and after the experiment.

5. *General problems cannot be solved, but specific problems can always be solved.* If there is one ultimate truth about solving problems, this is it. Generalities are nice to talk about, but trying to correct a broad problem is an exercise in futility unless it is broken into its separate parts. General problems are not problems at all, but merely symptoms.

For this reason, nothing can be done about productivity directly, other than to work harder, which is not always possible. However, a great deal can be done about specific problems such as an unreliable machine or unclear repair orders.

The important thing to remember is that low productivity or quality is a symptom of a number of diseases and not a disease in itself. Treating a disease cures the patient; treating the symptoms only provides temporary relief. That is why many attempts to improve performance only give temporary results.

If you want to improve productivity and quality, you need to solve the nitty-gritty problems that occur throughout the plant or office. To do that, you must be able to identify and measure the specific causes of problems so the Scientific Method can be used in solving them.

6. *Big problems are noticed and corrected, while small ones become accepted and ignored.* Consider what happens when the main computer in a bank breaks down. The failure is noticed immediately and everything is done to fix the problem. In a matter of a few hours it is running again. However, if that same computer loses five minutes every hour because of bad input data or operator errors, over several weeks it will lose more productive time for those reasons than it will ever lose from catastrophic failures. Nobody will notice this lost time because:

   • The operators see all the little interferences as "normal" because they've been going on for years;
   • Some of the problems are infrequent and are considered to be exceptions instead of recurring problems which can be treated; and,
   • Because the problems are spread over a large number of people and a long period of time, no one can see their total cost.

   A consequence of the proposition that small problems go unnoticed is: *When you're trying to improve performance, don't waste time looking for the big problems, because they have probably been solved a long time ago.* Disheartening, isn't it? Don't be discouraged. There is a lot more potential in the small problems than ever existed in the big ones anyway. Remember, very little gold is mined as one pound nuggets; most of it comes from fine dust. Anyone would like to find the one magic key that will increase performance 50 percent, but it doesn't exist. At least no one has found it yet.

On rare occasions, a new machine or method can make a significant difference, but this doesn't happen very often — and when it does, the problem was usually obvious in the first place. Breakthroughs do happen, but most of the time, big problems are the result of many little problems.

In a large photofinishing laboratory, where productivity was doubled in a five-year period, no single action accounted for more than one or two percentage points of improvement. Most of the quality problems had an initial error rate in the range of a few tenths of 1 percent. At the beginning of the program, no one dreamed of reaching the quality and productivity levels finally achieved. Yet, by reducing already low error rates for about 200 variables, outstanding results were achieved. *Most importantly, the results were permanent because the production process was improved and the control systems were in place to make sure it stayed that way.*

7. *Almost all problems in a business are recurring.* Truly random events such as lightning bolts or catastrophic equipment failures do happen, but nothing can be done about them. However, most problems in a business happen over and over again at a reasonably predictable rate. In most cases, what appears to be random is actually only infrequent. That is a big difference. Unlike random events, something can be done to control recurring problems because there is an underlying cause within the production system which can be treated.

8. *Nearly every person will do their best if they are treated with respect, given the proper tools, and rewarded for their performance.* Sure, there are some people who try to

do as little as possible, but they are so few they're hardly worth mentioning. This doesn't mean employees don't have to be trained and managed, but if you don't accept this proposition, you're defeated before you start.

If you assume that people are always most of the problem, it follows that the only way to improve performance is to work harder and make no mistakes. That severely limits the variables you can change in your search for better performance.

Although there are many technical aspects to productivity and quality, everything happens through people. It is possible to run a profitable business by treating people as objects, but don't expect to do as well as you could.

*Motivated people will find a way to make something work.
Indifferent people will only do what they are told. Threatened
people will look for reasons to fail.*

Summary

The basic principles that form the foundation of a successful quality and productivity improvement program are few in number and simple in concept. These principles have been used by successful managers for a long time, but they are often ignored or forgotten. Find a business with low performance or a failed attempt to improve productivity and you will find one or more of these elements missing. Build your program to improve quality and productivity on this foundation and success is virtually assured.

CHAPTER 2

Productivity, Quality, and Performance

Understanding Productivity

In spite of all the attention given to productivity, the true meaning of the word has been generally overlooked. *Most people assume "productivity" means units per labor hour, and most people are wrong.* Costs are always important, but in most companies, having the lowest direct labor cost is not the reason for their success. For example, one survey of small to mid-sized manufacturing firms showed that product quality and service were much more important than the cost of the products.[5] A few other examples are IBM and Compaq Computer — rather successful companies not known for having the lowest priced products.

In manufacturing companies, direct labor costs are certainly important, but they are steadily shrinking as a percentage of the total cost of bringing a product to a customer. The average direct labor cost of sales for manufacturers is rarely above 15 percent. General and administrative labor costs are usually higher than that. Most companies are not as direct labor intensive as they think they are.

Taking a narrow-minded viewpoint on productivity or quality ignores other issues which may be far more important. Factors such as short order lead times, on-time deliveries, being able to handle a complex product mix, and high quality can be much more important in the marketplace. Working on the wrong priorities will waste resources and miss opportunities. *Any efforts to improve productivity must be directed at increasing the total performance of a business, not just the performance of a few of its parts.* That must start with the customer.

An example of what total productivity means was expressed by a CEO of a very successful textile company. During a plant tour he said:

> "If you compare our plant to the way the experts say it should be built, you will wonder how we stay in business. It's a hodgepodge of equipment and not very efficient by conventional standards. But it lets us give our customers what they want, when they want it, at a reasonable price. It works, but sometimes I wonder why."

As measured by units per labor hour, this plant might not rank as one of the best, but in terms of total company productivity, it is a winner. There is no question why it works — it is designed to meet its customers' needs in terms of product, quality, and service at a competitive price. And this CEO is crazy like a fox.

Productivity is defined as output divided by input. Simple enough, but the big question is: "What output do you want?" A better question is: "What outputs do your customers want?" After all, if you are efficiently making what the market doesn't want, that can hardly be considered productive. It follows that the first step to determining what productivity means for your business is to decide who your customers are and what they want. No company is big enough to be all things to all people.

This does not mean a detailed strategic plan must be prepared in order to improve performance. It does mean that corporate objectives and the strategies to achieve them must be clearly defined and understood by everyone. For energies to be focused, you first need a target. As someone once put it:

Nothing is more wasteful
than doing with great efficiency
that which is totally unnecessary.

Most importantly, what the customer wants must be understood and satisfied. This is not a trivial point. There are many cases where attempts to improve productivity have resulted in disaster because the company did not understand what was important to its customers and itself. One company thought their national sales staff was productive if they opened new accounts. They opened so many they became their own worst competitor. Profit margins shrank and so did the company.

At the department level, falling into the trap of thinking only in terms of units/hour can be equally dangerous. It is likely to lead to conflicts and bottlenecks, resulting in higher costs and lower output for the company as a whole. Of course, being as efficient as possible is always desirable, but only as long as it does not conflict with higher level objectives.

According to Wickham Skinner, "The very way mangers define productivity improvement and the tools they use to achieve it push their goal further out of reach." He maintains that while improving efficiency and reducing waste is always important, it is not enough to gain a competitive edge because of the advantage other countries have in low cost labor.[6]

Some executives maintain that conventional cost accounting and using cost reduction as the only justification for investment is wrecking American business.[7] Executives looking at return on investment need to realize there are other returns that may be more important cost savings.

I can't vouch for the impact on American business, but as I write this, two companies come to mind that would be much better off if their labor costs were a little higher and they could ship their products when they promised. Oddly enough, if they focused on reducing order cycle time instead of costs, they would probably find productivity increasing as well.

Be careful what you ask for,
because you will probably get it.

Productivity is a simple concept. In the narrow sense it is the ratio of output to input and measures how efficiently resources are used. But in broader terms, what you really want as an output may take some thought — especially when there are several desirable outputs. From a company perspective, the customer ultimately determines whether a company's efforts are productive or not.

If you want to improve productivity, the first thing to do is make sure you are going after the right outputs — what your customer wants. Then, and only then, should you begin to work on doing them as efficiently as possible. Thinking only in terms of labor efficiency will make you blind to more important opportunities.

Understanding Quality

"Quality" has several meanings depending on the customer's needs and wants. Recognized quality factors for a physical product are listed below.[8]

- *Performance* — How well something does what it is supposed to do.
- *Features* — How many options, bells, and whistles a product has.
- *Reliability* — The mean time between failures.
- *Conformance* — How well the product meets its specifications.
- *Durability* — How long the product lasts.
- *Serviceability* — How easily a product can be repaired.

- *Aesthetics* — Looks, feel, and "sex appeal."
- *Perception* — Image, as opposed to real qualities.

For services, quality has other dimensions: [9]

- *Tangibles* — What the customer sees in people, facilities, and equipment. Similar to "aesthetics" for a product.
- *Reliability* — Being able to perform the service dependably and consistently. Doing what you say you will do.
- *Responsiveness* — Promptness and willingness to help customers.
- *Assurance* — Ability of the company's representatives to convey trust and confidence through knowledge and courtesy.
- *Empathy* — Conveying a caring attitude by providing individualized attention to customers.

The tricky part about services is that "quality" is greatly affected by a customer's expectations. These can vary from customer to customer even though the service performed may be consistent. Raise expectations too high and quality may be seen as poor, even if a good service was provided. That can apply to products as well.

Many companies provide both products and services, so any combination of these dimensions of quality might be important for a business. Of course, what matters most depends on the customer. In the ideal situation, what is delivered conforms to the specification and exceeds the customer's expectations.

These quality factors can be lumped into two broad categories — *design quality* and *execution quality*. Design quality reflects the functions, features, and aesthetics of a product, such as whether a chair is made out of leather or plastic.

Increasing design quality generally raises product costs because better materials, more materials, and more labor are required in the product. No one has yet found a way to make a Mercedes for the same cost as a Ford.

Execution or conformance quality reflects how well a product meets its specifications. Two products could be very different in terms of design quality but could be essentially the same in terms of conformance quality. For example, a Taurus might compare very well with a Mercedes in terms of execution quality but not in design quality. In this book, quality of conformance is the only concern. Hereafter, "quality" means conformance to requirements. But that definition is valid only if the requirements reflect what the customer wants. Unless the customer is satisfied, nothing else matters.

Who determines a product's requirements? The intended use certainly has an influence, but ultimately the customer defines a product's requirements by voting with his or her pocketbook. Engineers and marketing people may think they determine product requirements, but in the long run, they only translate customers' wants into something more specific. Ultimately, quality is measured in terms of customer satisfaction, not conformance to a specification.

What is not often realized, however, is that there are many more customers in a production system than the person paying the bill. We all have customers. They are the people who receive our goods and services. Department B may be the customer of department A; Manufacturing is the customer of Engineering, and so on. These customers, having different needs, will have different ways of defining quality.

Customers outside a company usually have options for filling their needs. If they can't get what they want from one vendor, they can usually go to another. Internal customers, on the other hand, usually have no place else to go and must make do with what they get or negotiate for what they need.

For example, if Engineering is not providing proper drawings to Manufacturing, complaints from the Manufacturing supervisors are likely to be countered with the reply:

> "Nobody's perfect. I'm sure Engineering is doing the best they can. Just correct the errors and make do with what you have. That's what you're getting paid for."

Of course, this doesn't correct the problem; it just gets buried deep enough so everyone can pretend it isn't there. After employees are told several times to ignore the problems, it should hardly be surprising that is exactly what happens. The problems become a normal part of the job, and everyone thinks they are productive because they are working so hard compensating for them.

Like rot in an apple, this kind of thinking spreads throughout a company until everyone is spending a big part of their time correcting others' mistakes. Nobody wants to cause a problem for someone else (or themselves) by complaining too loudly, so the problems persist. Some examples of this behavior are: (1) Accounts Receivable trying to collect from bad accounts because salesmen didn't follow credit procedures; (2) production line workers trying to use tools that don't work; and (3) shipments being delayed because shipping instructions are incomplete.

Understanding that "quality" means conforming to requirements and that the customer is the source of these requirements is the first step on the road to improving the performance of any business function. The second step is to recognize that everyone is both a customer and a supplier in any business. When the quality requirements of internal customers aren't satisfied, the performance of a company suffers just as surely as when poor quality products and services are delivered to the person paying the bill.

The Relationship between Quality and Productivity

Quality and productivity are different dimensions of a higher level measure that could be called "performance" or "effectiveness." The word you use doesn't matter much. It does matter that you understand that the two factors are strongly related because they both come from the people and machines that make up a production system. This may be obvious, but what is not apparent to everyone is that productivity and quality have a direct relationship. *As quality increases, productivity increases — not the other way around.*

It is reasonable to think that lowering quality standards will increase productivity because the amount of "good" product made will increase slightly. If the specifications for the product were tighter than required by the customer, this could happen. But normally, it doesn't work that way.

When the customer's standards are not met, some of the defective products will be returned or will result in losing future sales. In all likelihood, this will eventually cost more than if the product wasn't sold in the first place. Trying to increase productivity by lowering quality standards is a losing game. The long term costs of poor quality products will always outweigh any short term gains. Unfortunately, the costs of poor quality are frequently invisible, so companies shooting themselves in the foot don't feel any pain.

These hidden costs were vividly demonstrated in a furniture company. Customers loved the design of the products but didn't care for lumps, wrinkles, and mismatched seams. During a discussion with one of the sales representatives, he stated:

> "You know, we don't really make sales calls any more. We approach the customer with our tail between our legs, wondering what complaints we're going to get hit with. By the time we get the customer pacified, it's time to leave and we don't get a chance to sell anything."

Look at the hidden costs in this example. Just making the sales call cost the company a minimum of $200 to $300. The opportunity cost of lost sales could be estimated from the customer's purchase history, but the lost contribution from one sales call could easily be $1000. Add to that the cost of processing the complaint, the cost of repair, and the cost of regaining the customer's confidence (how many calls will that take?) and you get a figure over $2000 very quickly. What shows on the accounting reports? Not a cent.

It also costs more to make a poor quality product than it does a good one. Low quality products are the result of bad design, untrained workers, unreliable equipment, and poor methods and procedures. Imagine a highly efficient plant or office — one that has skilled people, good equipment, and everything else that makes it run well. Now imagine this well-oiled system producing defective products or doing poor quality work. Difficult to do? Of course. It is a direct contradiction that a highly efficient organization will produce defective products.

Anyone who has managed a business or department knows from experience that when everything is running as it should be, quality, productivity and morale are at a high level. Throw in some bad raw material, a few machine problems, and some untrained people and you soon have productivity, product quality, and morale sinking rapidly together.

Don't make the mistake of thinking that just because your customers aren't complaining, you don't have quality problems. What the customer sees is one thing — how you are getting there is an entirely different matter.

Product quality and process quality are two different things. It is possible to have good product quality with low process quality by throwing away defective products, but that gets expensive. However, if the quality of the production process is improved by eliminating the problems within it, both product quality and productivity increase.

The High Costs of Low Quality

One reason why some people feel quality and productivity are in conflict is that they don't know what poor quality actually costs. These costs are underestimated because:

1. No one takes the time to estimate and add up all the costs. They are spread all over a company.
2. Some of the costs are opportunity costs and are not visible, as in the previous example of the furniture company.
3. Outside of waste and returns, conventional accounting systems do not report quality costs.
4. The additional work created by poor quality becomes accepted as standard procedure.

Statements like, "We always have to check the stock because the inventory report has so many errors," are signs of entrenched quality problems. *There is no natural law saying any process must generate a given level of defective products.* Is there any reason why some inventory counts must be incorrect? Or why some customers should be shipped a wrong product? Of course not.

Unfortunately, after operating with quality problems for a period of time, the current performance level becomes acceptable unless someone decides better results are possible. This willingness to live with a certain amount of poor quality work, by machines or people, is one characteristic that differentiates the Japanese from most American companies. American companies are more prone to be content when they're making money and the customer complaints aren't too loud. The Japanese philosophy is to "pursue the last grain of rice in the lunchbox."[10] Zero defects may never be achieved in a Japanese plant, but that is always the goal.

It is patently wrong thinking that any problem is not worth the effort to solve it. That kind of thinking only leads to the development of thousands of little problems that slowly bleed a company to death. Even if a minor improvement will not permit reducing staff or idling a machine, adding up these gains over time will eventually permit that to happen.

Estimating the costs of poor quality is important. If you believe it will cost more to improve quality than will be returned, then you will naturally stop trying to get better when quality gets to a comfortable level. On the other hand, if you know what poor quality is really costing you, you will probably get out your chopsticks and start scraping your own lunchbox.

For example, an air conditioning components manufacturer was experiencing order specification errors that often wouldn't be detected until the units were well into production. At final assembly, someone would discover that the control specified on the order was not compatible with the assembly. One of the part numbers was wrong, which would start the following chain of events: (1) work would halt on the shop floor while the production manager was notified; (2) the production manager would survey the situation and call the engineer; (3) the engineer would come out, scratch his head and call the sales manager to ask him to find out what the customer wanted; (4) this message would go to the branch office, then to the salesperson, then to the customer, and then to the customer's engineering firm to be resolved. (5) Once the problem was resolved, the information would flow back through most of the chain once more. At this point it might be discovered that the correct control was not in stock and wouldn't be available for at least three weeks.

Among other costs, the plant would lose production time, other orders would be delayed, a backorder would be created, and when the correct parts finally arrived, production would be interrupted once more to expedite the order. Then the assembly would probably be shipped air express because it was already late. Finally, future sales might be lost because of the customer's bad experience.

If you look closely at this example you will notice the following important points:

1. Everyone engaged in correcting the error is terribly busy but doing nothing that contributes to improving the output of the company. Their productivity is precisely zero.

2. The mistake is a recurring problem; therefore, something can be done to correct it. Unfortunately, each instance is considered an exception.

3. The impact of the error is distributed over many people, with each one seeing only a part of the problem. No one sees all the problems and costs created by one wrong number.

4. Most of the costs are not recognized by the accounting system. Many of the wasted hours would fall in the category of "overhead" and would not be noticed. The direct labor costs would not be assigned to a particular product. Since this was a recurring problem, weekly cost reports might not show anything unusual was happening. All that management would see was that for unexplained reasons, sales, direct costs, and overhead costs were creating lower profit margins than expected.

5. The cost of the problem increases greatly for both the customer and the company as time passes and as the work passes through the production system. If the error could be detected early in the process, the cost of correction would be relatively small. This is generally true of any quality problem.

If a value was assigned to the time spent correcting one of these problems, the cost of a single error would be at least several hundred dollars. It would be a fair bet that most people would be quite surprised by that figure and by how many errors were occurring every month. Combine the costs of all similar problems and the figure becomes very substantial. *Because the errors are not measured and the costs are invisible, no one takes action to eliminate them.*

Some studies have estimated that as much as 30 percent of a company's resources can be spent correcting quality problems that shouldn't happen in the first place. Based on my experience, those figures are quite reasonable. In one case, a detailed analysis showed the cost of remaking a product was $5.76 versus a cost of $0.72 for doing it right the first time. Roughly 35 percent of indirect and direct labor costs were being spent on correcting or compensating for quality problems. These problems occurred at many points in the production process and affected about 6 percent of the products. In other words, 35 percent of manufacturing labor costs were being spent on only 6 percent of the plant's production.

Failure to recognize the large impact of apparently small quality problems leads many managers to reach the wrong conclusion that big opportunities for increasing performance don't exist. When a small portion of poor quality work is consuming a large share of resources, improving quality increases productivity much more than is readily apparent.

In the following example, reducing rejects from 8 percent to 4 percent results in an increase in labor productivity of 27 percent. In practice, the gains would be greater over the long term because the resources spent correcting problems can be used where they can provide a better return. Fewer quality problems makes more management time available for training, solving problems, and the other things managers are supposed to do, instead of putting out daily fires.

Example: Assume a reject rate of 8 percent with 35 percent of available labor spent on all problems associated with rejects. If

100 hours were available and it took one hour to produce a unit, there would be 65 good units produced. Productivity would be 65 units/hour. Reducing the reject rate to 4 percent, increases the production rate of good units to 82.5 units/hour, increasing productivity by 17.5/65 = 27 percent.

8 percent rejects	*4 percent rejects*
65 good units	82.5 good units
35 lost hours	17.5 lost hours
100 hours	100 hours

This explains why there are so many examples of companies making productivity gains that far exceed their initial expectations.

It's not the 95 percent that's right that makes something work, it's the 5 percent that's wrong that messes everything up.

With a little reflection, you may be able to recall some days when everything went the way it should and productivity set new records. If so, you ought to ask yourself why that can't be done most of the time. Without extraordinary effort, what was once unusually good performance can become just another average day.

It Always Pays to Improve Quality

Perhaps the most damaging belief about quality is that there is some point where improving quality just doesn't pay. This is the same as saying at some point it doesn't pay to get better. Not many athletes would agree with that, but the belief persists in business that "good enough" is good enough.

In theory, when the incremental cost of improving quality gets greater than the incremental savings, it would not pay to make further improvements in quality. This argument is logically correct, but if that point exists, it is apparently so close to perfection that it is not a practical matter. It may never be possible to prove it always pays to improve the quality of a production process, but so far, there have been no reports to the contrary.

While it always pays to improve the quality of a process, it is definitely possible to have too much quality in a product from a design viewpoint. Whether or not a design feature or a tighter specification has any value is decided by the customer, not the vendor. That is one reason why understanding the customer's requirements, not just your specification, is so important.

Process quality costs may be in several forms such as material waste, rework costs, management time, and rejects. Product quality costs may show up as customer complaints, returns, and higher selling costs. *Whether it is process or product quality, poor quality always costs something*, as shown by Figure 2.1. Opportunity costs, such as lost sales, don't appear on an income statement, but it always pays to reduce them. The highest cost of all is a damaged reputation and the customer that never comes back. Ask GM, Ford, and Chrysler.

Any manager debating whether or not to improve quality is wasting his or her time. It is never a question of economics, assuming quality is increased by improving the production process. In the long run it is always better to improve quality and reap the rewards of higher productivity, lower costs, and satisfied customers. Saying that you can't afford to improve quality is the same as saying you can't afford to do it right the first time, but you can always afford to do it over. Unfortunately, in the increasingly competitive world market, your customer may never give you a second chance.

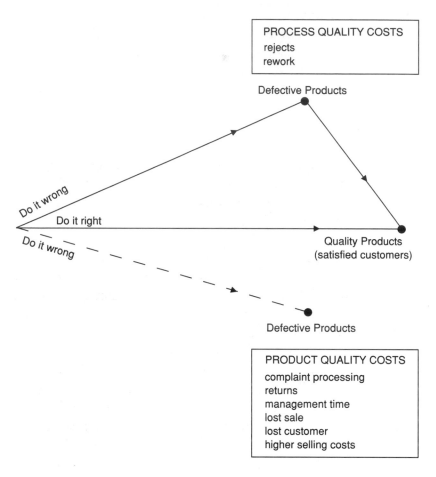

PROCESS QUALITY COSTS
rejects
rework

Defective Products

Do it wrong

Do it right

Do it wrong

Quality Products
(satisfied customers)

Defective Products

PRODUCT QUALITY COSTS
complaint processing
returns
management time
lost sale
lost customer
higher selling costs

Figure 2.1 Poor Quality Always Costs Something!

Summary

Productivity and quality are nearly synonymous because they are so directly related. They are two dimensions of what we call "performance." While it is important to understand the terms, it is not important to get hung up on semantics. When Japanese managers talk about "quality problems" in their operations they are as likely to be talking about inventory, scheduling, or absenteeism problems as about a product problem. Not only are all of these problems interrelated, they are considered to be problems in the management of the production process itself.[11]

Since most quality costs are not readily apparent it is easy for managers to think improving quality will increase costs. However, low productivity and high costs are not the result of high quality, but of poor quality throughout a production system— inadequate equipment, untrained and poorly motivated people, outdated methods, sloppy procedures and weak controls.

All productivity problems are ultimately caused by poor quality. Managers who want to improve productivity should not think only in terms of speeding up processes and making people work harder. Those are valid considerations, but managers will get better results if they start working on increasing the quality of raw materials, improving the reliability of equipment, improving the skills of people, and reducing the barriers to doing the job right the first time. When process quality increases, so does product quality and productivity.

CHAPTER 3

Performance Measurement and Performance Management

Management from an Information Perspective

To understand the relationship between performance measurement and performance management, let's take a look at the management process from an information perspective. As shown by Figure 3.1, the management process has four steps:

1. The *production process* creates products or services. The activities in the process generate data.
2. The *information system* takes the data and converts it to useful information. The terms "data" and "information" are often considered synonymous, but they are not. Data can be thought of as a collection of points or numbers, while information is the result of converting the data into a form that can be used for making a decision. Pages of numbers are data. When translated into a graph or summarized in some other fashion, the result is information.
3. The *decision-making system* analyzes the information it receives and makes decisions to allocate resources and take action.
4. The *organization* executes the decisions by taking action and using the resources allocated to it.

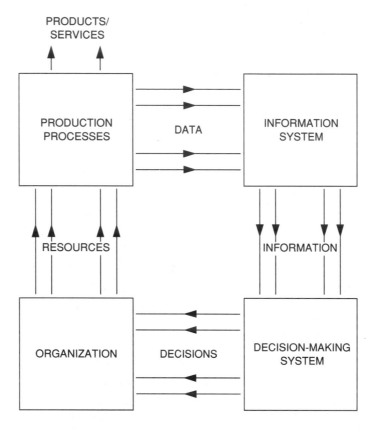

Figure 3.1 The Management Process

In the real world the parts of an actual management system interact and overlap in a complicated manner, but the model is a useful way of looking at the management process. Note that all parts of the system could have both manual and computer-based elements.

In any company there are many management systems and subsystems, both formal and informal. They all depend upon a steady flow of information as the basis for decisions. Where the formal systems do not supply the necessary information, informal systems will develop to fill the gaps as best they can. Just because people are making decisions doesn't mean they have the right information to make them.

If a company allocates its resources to the right places and uses them efficiently, it must achieve a high level of performance. Consequently, the performance of any company is the result of the decisions made by its managers. Since the quality of a decision is limited by the information available when it is made, *the performance of a business is directly related to the quantity and quality of information available to its managers.*

Obviously, the success of a business depends upon many other factors as well. Being in the market at the right time with the right product will cover just about any sin. In the long run, however, poor or incomplete information must result in bad decisions, wasted resources, and poor performance. To better understand this relationship, let's look at how information — specifically, performance measures — can improve performance.

Communicating Strategy and Clarifying Values

Every company has a strategy. In the best case, it is a conscious decision reflecting the company's chosen customers and how it will compete for them in the marketplace. In the worst case, it is simply doing whatever seems best at the time.

Assuming a company has a specific strategy, performance measures can be specified for every function reflecting that strategy. As mentioned earlier, this improves total productivity by focusing everyone's efforts on the same goal.

A well-defined system of performance measures also improves performance by providing a framework for making decisions. When managers clearly understand what is best for the company, the thousands of decisions that must be made every day will be better decisions. Without the proper frame of reference, some of these decisions will be based on false assumptions and personal values. A survey by Booz, Allen & Hamilton found that only 37 percent of senior officials felt new business goals were completely understood by other key managers. Worse yet, only 4 percent of the top bosses felt their middle managers totally understood.[12] Apparently the surveyors were afraid to go any lower than that.

A buyer, for instance, may have to consider the tradeoffs to make between price, product quality, delivery time, and vendor relations. What is most important — get the product delivered in two weeks or reduce costs by 2 percent? Similarly, a salesperson may have to decide which products to sell, the price, and even which customer to call on first. How should he or she allocate his time between new business and existing business? All sales dollars are not equal.

A biologist observed that every living organism survives because it has a competitive advantage in its environment. Businesses are no different. By translating strategy into specific terms, performance measures enhance the quality of decisions of all managers — from the executive suite to the shop floor. *If a company wants to "stick to its knitting," as recommended by Peters and Waterman,*[13] *it helps if everyone is working on the same pattern.* If everyone is not working toward the same goals, productivity has to suffer. Well-defined performance measures help keep everyone on the same track.

Identifying Problems and Opportunities

If increasing performance is seen as an exercise in identifying and solving problems, information must first be available to identify when problems are occurring. It is usually easier to ignore problems than solve them, but performance measures make it difficult to do that by making them visible.

Many managers find themselves in the position of a salesman who complained:

"Management wants to know why sales are down, but when I tell them about the quality and delivery problems with our best-selling products, nobody wants to listen."

With some hard numbers on quality and delivery performance, he might be heard — or proven wrong. In either case, appropriate action would be taken. In business, when there are differences of opinion about problems and no objective measures of performance, the person with less authority is automatically wrong. Even if he or she is right.

Objective performance measures help keep everyone honest,
even those who may not appreciate it.

Performance measures also keep problems in perspective. In one week, the average manager hears so many problems, complaints, and conflicting "facts," that he quickly gets mentally worn out and confused. In this condition, it is easy to start working on the wrong priorities. Consistent measures of performance help managers cut through the clutter and keep them focused on significant problems instead of emotional issues. By doing so, they help managers stay out of unproductive activity traps.

While problems may cause performance to be lower than normal, the presence of unrecognized opportunities may be signaled by performance being higher than normal. Managers should be as interested in opportunities as they are in problems, but they are more likely to bask in success than to ask why performance is so high. If productivity is high one day, what are the reasons? What must be done to make it happen more often? Performance measures can alert managers to opportunities as well as problems, but managers must ask questions and take action to convert opportunities to real benefits.

Where performance is not being measured,
it can almost certainly be improved.

Diagnosing Problems

When people say they have a problem such as a fever, a rough-running car, or thin profit margins, they are saying they feel symptoms. Solving problems will be discussed in more detail later, but the most important step in solving a problem is to identify the causes of the symptoms. To do this, you need to know how all the parts that make up the production system are acting. While subjective information can be helpful, it can be very misleading. Performance measures are the only way to get consistent objective information.

Understanding the Process

To improve quality and productivity, you must improve the process producing the goods or services. How can you improve something you don't understand? Not very well. Like an amateur mechanic, trying to fix something you don't understand may result in disaster. Performance measures enable managers to see relationships between variables, providing them with insight into how their production system works that cannot be obtained from any other source.

Whether you are trying to establish a Just-In-Time manufacturing system or improve response time to service calls, if you don't understand how the present system works, you stand a good chance of shooting yourself in the foot.

Allocating Resources Efficiently

For a company to get the most out of its limited resources, its manpower and money should be allocated according to the upside potential or downside risk in each functional area. Being aware of problems and opportunities is not enough. Managers also need to have some idea of their relative importance. Obviously, quantitative information is required. Accurate measures of value rarely exist for problems and opportunities, but useful estimates can be made with good performance measures and accounting information.

Subjective information will be part of almost every decision to allocate resources, but performance measures will help put the options in perspective. Managers who rely on "gut feeling" for making such decisions will find they are often responding only to something they should have avoided at dinner.

Defining Responsibility

In spite of job descriptions that would make a Washington lawyer turn green with envy, there are millions of managers who don't really understand what they are supposed to do other than keep the boss happy. Informal surveys taken at seminars indicate this is a major problem. A formal survey of top and middle managers showed that while "clear performance goals" and "good, fair performance measures" were important to 80 percent of them, only 40 percent felt these conditions were satisfied.[14]

Upper level managers generally have some performance measures such as market share, sales, profits, and return on investment which partly define their responsibility. Even though these measures may be incomplete or not the best choice, at least the executives have a clear definition of "good" and "bad" performance. They wouldn't like it if they didn't have these measures as a guide, but they readily put their subordinates in the awkward position of having to guess what they are supposed to accomplish.

Most job descriptions define responsibilities and tasks but don't say what "good performance" means. Performance measures can make that very clear and also be a constant reminder of what matters most. They should be part of every job description.

Improving Control and Planning

When we say managers are "in control," we generally mean that they understand the situation and are taking the proper corrective action. In other words, for a given input they can predict the output and react accordingly.

It also means they should be able to make reasonably accurate projections of the future when internal or external forces change. Typical questions faced by managers are:

- What will manufacturing need to do to accommodate an 18-percent increase in orders in a product line?
- How might introducing a new product affect customer service?
- How many salespeople will be required to service a new region?

Perfect answers to questions like these are not possible, but by knowing how the company was affected by similar changes in the past and how the production system behaves, good estimates can be made instead of wild guesses. The ability of managers to make projections and meet them is a very good indicator of how well they understand the activities they are managing.

Understanding how a production system works and the forces that affect costs is necessary for good budgeting and financial planning. Budgets should not be simply an extrapolation of what happened last year. Not understanding the relationship between activities and costs can lead to unpleasant surprises.

A case in point was a human resources department that was 25 percent over its budget, which was based on a fixed percentage of sales. Although budgeting on the basis of sales seemed reasonable at first glance, it had no relationship to reality. The primary variables driving costs were the number of positions to be filled, the type of positions, the percentage of acceptance, the distance from headquarters to new stores, and the demands made on the department for services. While there was a strong correlation between these variables and sales in the past, there was no direct cause/effect relationship.

In addition to the time spent chasing a problem that didn't exist, the bad budget created morale problems. The department was being accused of being inefficient even though productivity had actually increased. Everyone in the department knew they were working harder and getting further behind, but they couldn't explain why.

When the situation was explained and the *causes* of the cost increases were understood, opportunities for improving productivity by 30 percent were identified and implemented.

Budgets which are not based on well-understood
relationships between activities and costs
are poor indicators of performance.

Identifying When and Where Action Is Needed

If managers are going to have good control, they must know when and where to take corrective action. To do this, they need to know (1) how the production system is currently performing and (2) what normal performance looks like. Without performance measurement, deciding what needs attention must be based on subjective judgment.

We mere humans are limited in our ability to remember and process data. When we rely on subjective judgment, problems are frequently not recognized until it is too late: product quality slips until sales fall off, inventory increases until the warehouse is full, or backlogs increase until customers start screaming about late shipments. Solving the problem then becomes the number one priority. A crash program gets the situation under control and everyone breathes a sigh of relief. Meanwhile, lurking beneath the surface another crisis is slowly taking shape. Without timely performance measures, problems must often reach catastrophic proportions before they can be seen.

Problems that are ignored never go away by themselves — they only grow until they get so big they cannot be ignored.

Guiding and Changing Behavior

Performance measures play two vital roles in developing people and organizations. As already mentioned, by clarifying and communicating what good performance means, they guide thinking and efforts into the right channels.

Secondly, they accelerate individual and group development by providing constant feedback. Improving skills and changing behavior is a learning process that doesn't happen overnight. It typically takes months for a person to learn basic skills in any position and a year or two to learn all the little details that make the difference between acceptable and excellent performance.

Many instances of feedback can be required just to correct a single problem. Without good performance information, feedback will be infrequent and probably confusing. The messages sent will depend upon what happens to get noticed instead of what is important. Consequently, the whole learning process will suffer.

People learn, but they "unlearn" also. Because of turnover and "unlearning," the fully trained organization that exists today can look quite a bit different a year from now. The only way to make training stick is to make feedback about performance an integral part of day-to-day operations.

How quickly performance can deteriorate was shown in a plant where certain rejects had been reduced to absolutely zero for several months. Thinking the problem was eliminated, management quietly removed the control graph for this factor (let's call it "dirty rollers") from the weekly results package, but did not stop collecting data should any incidents occur.

About six weeks later, rejects at the plant were increasing for no apparent reason. Being suspicious, management checked the raw data for "dirty roller" rejects. Sure enough, rejects had stayed at zero for two weeks and then began to increase. In six weeks, they had grown totally out of control.

The graph was quickly reinstated and in a few weeks, defects were back to zero. Needless to say, the graph became a permanent fixture in the reporting package.

The lesson to be learned from this unplanned experiment is that when "dirty rollers" was removed from the charts, a message was sent that this problem was no longer important. If it didn't matter to management, it surely wasn't important to the operators. Similar experiences are easy to find. [15]

What gets measured becomes important —
that's why it gets done.

Making Accomplishments Visible

How would you like the following job? You go to work and do pretty much the same thing every day - - with the exception of an occasional crisis thrown in for aggravation's sake. At the end of each day, week, or month you can't see any tangible result of your efforts. The parts, memos, or phone calls that you produced will have moved on and you will never see them again.

Once a year your manager calls you into his office for a "performance review" which probably doesn't do much more than confirm the fact that you worked the past year without creating too many problems. In fact, if you did your job well, you'll probably get fewer positive strokes than if you were a problem child and improved your performance!

You don't know what is happening in the company or why changes are made in schedules or products. Even though you see many problems in the company and the department, your complaints are ignored. You are rarely asked for your opinion, given the opportunity to offer suggestions, or participate in even the smallest decision.

In exchange for being treated like an animated vegetable, you are expected to look forward to working each day and do your best at whatever needs doing for the company's sake (smiling all the time, of course).

Does this sound exciting? For the average worker, and many managers as well, this is a fairly accurate description of their jobs. No wonder workers are alienated. This doesn't just apply to the United States, it is a universal problem. Thomas H. Naylor, an economist at Duke University, contends the Soviet Union and the United States are not that much different as far as alienation of the worker is concerned. In his opinion, that alienation is one of the primary targets of perestroika, and "America also needs perestroika, but we are simply too arrogant to admit it."[16]

Managers are no different in one sense than the customer service representative or the fork-lift operator in the warehouse: all take pride in accomplishing something. Most people, whatever their rank, want to enjoy a sense of accomplishment from their work.[17] Unfortunately, many jobs simply don't provide the opportunity for people to see their individual achievements. Performance measures can overcome this problem by making visible what is otherwise invisible.

The power of making performance visible was demonstrated somewhat by accident in a company that had problems with the accuracy of its inventory records. To improve the inventory system, logic checks were built into the computer programs to detect probable errors and kick them out for review and corrective action.

Part of the plan was to give the department manager some training and support along with holding him responsible for reducing the errors. His initial reaction was not exactly enthusiastic, because now his performance was visible and he was clearly accountable: somewhat threatening when you're used to just doing tasks and putting out fires all day.

However, something unexpected happened when the first daily report came out. Everyone in the department was amazed to see they had processed 3,000 transactions the day before. The manager took me aside and said: "You know, I think this is going to work out. The guys were surprised to see what they did yesterday. Many of them have worked here for years, and this is the first time they can see what they've accomplished."

It took only a few weeks and a little progress for everyone to get excited about reducing inventory errors also. A graph showing daily transaction volume and the error rate was posted right beside the stock pickup window for everyone to see. Error reduction quickly became a bragging point for everyone in the department. In four months, errors were reduced from 5 percent of transactions to a few tenths of 1 percent.

Reducing errors was the goal. Making performance visible and providing constant feedback was the means. Employee involvement was the ultimate key to success. The employees had to accept changes to procedures and they were also the source of many improvements to the system. They supported the program because (1) they understood why errors had to be reduced, (2) they weren't blamed for the problem, (3) they were given the chance to contribute, (4) they could see what they accomplished, and (5) they were given assistance, not criticism, in solving the problems.

A very important benefit of performance measures is that the effect of incremental improvements becomes visible even when each change may be so small that its impact would not be apparent. By showing the combined impact of minor changes, everyone can see their value. This positive feedback makes people aware that little things count and also provides an incentive to do more.

Getting Everyone Involved

Companies want their employees to "get involved" and "be part of the team," but they don't provide any way for them to feel like more than cogs in a machine. Performance measures make it possible for employees and managers alike to feel a sense of individual and group accomplishment.

They also offer managers an opportunity to have more meaningful and specific communication with employees. If you say, "Give me some ideas about how to improve performance," the statement is so broad that not much useful conversation can take place. But if you say, "Let's talk about why we're having errors in the labeling operation," the chances of getting a fruitful discussion started are much better.

A manufacturing vice president bragged that he made a point of walking through the shop every day "to create the right image with the troops." Unfortunately, the only conversation during his daily walk was a bunch of time-worn cliches. No real communication ever took place — a fact very apparent to everyone. Being able to ask a few specific, timely questions would have greatly improved both his credibility and productivity.

In the same vein, the story is told of a young man named Jim who rose from the shop floor to become president. On his annual tour of the plants, he would always take the time to visit one of his old buddies. As part of the ritual, they would flip a coin for a cigar. When asked how this attention made him feel, the old-timer replied: "Well, I think it's kind of silly, but it's really no big deal. He's got a lot of problems as president. If it makes Jim happy, I'm glad to do it."

Like Jim, managers who spend much of their time performing superficial stunts should ask themselves who is motivating whom. Don't take this the wrong way. Publicity and hype are important, but if they are not backed by substance, they only treat symptoms. There is some value to "Management By Wandering Around" as described by Peters and Waterman,[18] but "Wandering Around With A Purpose" should also be part of every manager's routine.

Having well-defined issues which need attention also makes it possible to broaden the base of people working on them. Individuals, teams, and supervisors can be assigned (or volunteer) to tackle problems in their area of responsibility. This gives them the opportunity to make decisions and also be recognized for making a specific contribution. Can you imagine how good it feels to be asked to help solve a problem when you have never been asked before?

Being involved and being in on things ranks higher than good wages for most workers (assuming they feel their current wages are fair).[19] Performance measures, if used properly, are a powerful catalyst for creating real communication links throughout a business. They provide managers a basis for asking questions, recognizing achievement, and stimulating discussion. Performance measures not only help get employees involved, they help get managers involved as well.

Want to get all your employees involved? Here's all you need to do:

1. TELL them what you want to accomplish and why.
2. TELL them what's in it for them.
3. TELL them what they need to do to achieve the objectives.
4. ASK them what their problems are and what might solve them.
5. LISTEN to what they have to say.
6. HELP them develop solutions.
7. RECOGNIZE their efforts and accomplishments.
8. REWARD their performance in a tangible manner as you promised.

9. TREAT everybody with the same respect you would like to receive. The Golden Rule may be centuries old, but it still works.

This isn't a complicated process. The hardest part is changing old beliefs and habits. Some individuals may need help in changing their attitudes and polishing their skills, but most managers are already well-equipped to get their employees and themselves involved in improving performance. In my opinion, the *individual worker and first-line supervisor/manager are the most under-utilized resources in businesses today.* Performance measurements can be the key to unlocking much of that potential — providing they are used as a key and not as a club.

Making Delegation Easy and Effective

It is every manager's job to delegate responsibility, but some don't do it very well. They want to make all the decisions and solve all the problems. This robs the manager of valuable time and his or her people of the chance to grow.

No doubt, some managers don't delegate because of a strong need for control and power. But the biggest reasons seem to be fear and distrust — fear that the job won't get done and a lack of trust in the person to do it well.

Delegating is like turning the reins of a horse over to a novice. It's easier to do if you can still see where you're headed so you can grab the reins if necessary. By letting managers "see" where departments are headed, performance measures let managers loosen the reins and still keep control.

A case in point was a small company where the CEO had unconsciously fallen into the trap of doing everything himself. He was the biggest bottleneck in the company but didn't realize it. The managers were frustrated because they couldn't make any decisions and progress was moving at a snail's pace. When this was brought to his attention, the reply was, "But if I'm not involved in all the decisions, I don't know what's going on."

A logistics and performance measurement system which gave him a timely and thorough picture of what was happening from order entry through shipping solved the problem. He was also told he had to choose one of three options: stop growing, go crazy, or delegate.

A few weeks later, when asked how everything was running he replied: "Great! Ed and the other managers have made all kinds of improvements. Those guys can do a lot more than I have been giving them credit for."

When you let go of the reins,
a team of horses usually runs faster.

Performance measures let managers see what is happening while keeping their distance. Only a fool would be willing to delegate and be kept in the dark. Few managers are fools, but the evidence indicates that delegation is a weak point in many companies. Managers who don't delegate work harder, accomplish less, and don't develop themselves or their organization as they should. Without good feedback on performance, effective delegation is nearly impossible.

If a manager has a good performance measurement system, he or she should be able to take a vacation for a few weeks and be able to tell, within thirty minutes of returning: (1) how well the department performed overall, (2) where problems occurred, and (3) exactly who needs to be talked to first.

Rewarding Performance

Managers always talk about rewarding performance, but if you're not measuring performance, it is more likely that appearances will be rewarded instead of accomplishment.

However, since accomplishment results from effort, it is important to reward effort also — but not if it is the wrong kind of effort. For example, a shift manager who appeared to be a human dynamo earned a reputation as a "real hustler." But when his quality and productivity performance measures were evaluated, it became clear that his frenzied activity was not a sign of useful hard work, but of poor organization, planning, and delegation.

What you see isn't always what you're getting.
Performance measures put people as well as problems in perspective.

Having specific performance measures in place helps assure that the right kind of behavior is rewarded. As a manager at Hewlett-Packard put it, "We used to reward people for putting out fires. Now we reward them for avoiding problems in the first place."[20] Just as managers want clear performance goals, they want their own pay tied to their performance. Only about half of the managers in a survey said this was happening in their case.[21]

Recognizing Performance

Good performance can be rewarded with bonuses and raises, but a more important form of reward costs absolutely nothing. It is simple recognition. While we take pleasure in achieving something, we take more pleasure in having others recognize us for it.

Referring back to the inventory control example, everyone in the department was proud of reducing errors, but if management's enthusiasm did not match theirs, interest would have quickly faded. It is significant to note that in this case, no one was told they would get an increase in pay, a bonus, or promotion for reducing errors. Instead, they were told that it was their job, why it was important, and how their performance would affect both the company's and their long-term success.

Money is important if someone feels he or she is not being paid fairly, but it isn't generally a positive motivator.[22] Simply paying people more will not get them to improve their performance. Offering incentives based on performance sometimes works, but often the gains are short-lived for two reasons: (1) the performance measures are not valid and (2) management expects to improve performance by getting everyone to work harder and better, instead of finding ways to improve the production process. If most people are already working as hard as they can, the gains that can be realized purely from more effort are quite limited.

Summary

Performance measurement is essential for achieving and maintaining high levels of productivity and quality, for good management control and planning, and for developing and motivating an organization. But all things considered, the most valuable benefit of proper performance measures is a sound understanding of how the production system works and the forces that drive it.

Managers without performance measures for their areas of responsibility are like travelers without a map, pilots flying blind, or doctors without a stethoscope—they are working harder and accomplishing less than they otherwise could. Being a manager is difficult enough without working with a handicap.

If you want to manage performance,
you must measure performance.

CHAPTER 4

Key Performance Factors

The Balancing Act

Achieving "maximum performance" or something close to it should be every company's objective, but the hard fact of life is that you can't have it all. No company has the resources to be all things to all people and some desirable objectives are inherently conflicting.

For example, in manufacturing, tradeoffs must be made between inventory, machine utilization, capacity, productivity, customer service, and response time. "Just-In-Time" production may appear to be the answer to all those problems, but JIT systems also may have the limitation of not being able to quickly respond to changes in demand.

In sales, it may be necessary to balance the selling of established products with introducing new products. In a service company, it may be necessary to balance response time with utilization of personnel. Even in our daily lives, most of us mere mortals have to balance many conflicting interests. Business is certainly no different.

Without a clear definition of company strategy and what "performance" means for each department to support that strategy, there is a real danger of "suboptimization," or of spending $1.15 to save $1.00. This occurs when department objectives are not consistent with the needs of the total company and each other. *Maximum performance of the whole does not result from trying to independently maximize the performance of each of the parts.*

For example, if we took the best parts out of several different automobiles and tried to put them together, we would not wind up with the best car in the world. In fact, it wouldn't even run. Interestingly enough, in the 1930s Toyota made a truck by using all the "best" components at the time — a Ford chassis, a Chevrolet engine, and a Chrysler DeSoto body. The first one broke down on the way to the showroom and it took years to overcome the problems.[23]

The problem of suboptimization seems obvious when talking about cars, but it is common to see companies trying to achieve minimum inventories, maximum units/labor hour, maximum machine utilization, minimum production cycle times, and maximum customer service. Then they try to grab any order they can get to maximize sales. In the real world it is impossible to maximize everything; trying to do so will only maximize everyone's stress.

The negative effects of asking for everything should not be taken lightly. When one department maximizes its performance, it may limit the performance of other departments. This can result in organizational conflicts as well as lower quality and higher costs.

Achieving maximum performance is a balancing act, not a simple problem of optimizing one variable. Management must determine the most important factors for the entire company and assign departmental objectives and performance measures which are consistent with them. It is not terribly difficult to define departmental objectives and constraints so they are in harmony with each other and the total company. When this is not done, the result is lower performance for the company and discouraged employees who know they are being asked to play a game they can't win.

When defining what "performance" means, the entire company must be addressed as a unit, not as a set of independent parts. The production process starts when the customer places an order, so that the production system includes everything from taking the order to delivering the product. Every link in the chain needs to be considered.

This does not mean that improving the performance of a manufacturing division or a customer service department cannot be treated as a separate project. It does mean that the relationship of a department to the company and its customers must first be examined to make sure the measures of productivity and quality for the department will be consistent with the company's objectives.

For any production system to achieve maximum productivity in the broad sense, its capabilities must be consistent within itself and with what its customers want. Salespeople can't be promising orders in four weeks when the customers want them in two and the plant can't fill them in less than six. That is why having key performance factors at the company and department level which are compatible and well-understood by everyone is so important.

Company Key Performance Factors

A company's success depends upon many internal and external variables. Inevitably, these interacting forces reduce to a few critical factors that make the difference between success and failure.

A company's key performance factors (or measures) could include both quality and productivity measures. Some possible company key performance factors are given below. The possibilities are endless. They are a direct outgrowth of the strategy the business uses to survive in the marketplace. By definition, the number of key performance factors is limited — three might be an average number and five would seem to be an absolute maximum. Note that unless a company's strategy is to be the lowest cost producer, manufacturing costs and direct labor costs may not be key factors. This does not mean they aren't important, but it does mean these costs should not always be the primary focus of management's attention.

A Sample of Key Performance Factors

Average order cycle time
Percentage of orders shipped when promised
Time to introduce a new product
Percentage of incoming telephone call "hang-ups"
Customer repeat frequency
Plant or equipment utilization
Average time to respond to a service order

One company that understands the importance of knowing its key performance factors is IJ Companies, a foodservice distributor. Because the company observed that incomplete orders was one of the top three complaints on numerous customer surveys, they decided that shipping orders 100 percent complete would be a top priority. This could be measured by line items shipped short as a percentage of total items ordered.

Understanding what their customers wanted, they improved their order processing and inventory system to improve the service level from 98 percent to 99.9 percent. The benefits were happier customers, increased sales, and increased profits.[24]

It appears that in a majority of companies, the important factors are subconsciously understood but not stated in specific terms.[25] It pays to be specific. If you don't know where you're going, others can't help you get there and you may wind up in a very uncomfortable place.

No company has the resources to be all things to all people. Every company has critical success factors whether it recognizes them or not. Without areas where it tries to excel and will not compromise, a business lacks the driving force that will make it great.

Focusing only on the bottom line
causes management myopia.

Department Key Performance Measures

Like companies, departments should also have key performance factors. Poorly defined key performance factors result in goals that keep changing from week to week. One week the cry goes out: "Cut inventories!" Next week it is: "Increase customer service!" or "Cut back on overtime!" Every week the game changes, leaving everyone totally confused. This "shifting sands" or "moving target" behavior is a sure sign of poor management control and wasted effort.

With constantly changing goals, holding someone accountable for results becomes pointless. How do you hold someone responsible for the score when you haven't told them the rules of the game? Not that this doesn't prevent some managers from trying. As one frustrated department manager told his Division VP in a meeting: "I'll be glad to dig the ditch any way you want, but please just tell me how long, how wide, and which darn direction! "

In all of the discussion about Japanese productivity, one of the primary reasons for their success is often overlooked. That is, their top management takes seriously their responsibility for setting consistent long-term goals toward which even short-term decisions can be directed. This lets all manufacturing managers understand the strategic significance of their day-to-day operational decisions.[26] In other words, they know where the company is headed, the heading doesn't change every day, and they can make decisions which support the company's long-term goals.

Of course, the Japanese aren't the only ones who understand the importance of clearly defined values and priorities. A small manufacturer of premium-priced furniture expressed it this way:

> "I know what business we're in. We make top-of-the-line products and deliver when we promise. We never compromise quality and everyone here knows it. Of course, I want to be as efficient as possible, but if there is ever a question about the product, we correct the problem or throw the piece out."

How many companies can make a similar well-defined statement of their business? No doubt, many can. But it is clear many cannot — or else, after achieving some degree of success, they forget what made them successful.

Once the company key factors have been determined, the key performance measures for departments can be defined. Figure 4.1 illustrates the relationship between strategy and key performance measures.

Figure 4.2 is an example of the key performance factors for a company and its major departments. In this case, it is assumed that reducing order cycle time and meeting delivery commitments would increase sales and profits. Consequently, processing time and delays should be measured throughout the production process, including such departments as order entry, engineering, purchasing, manufacturing, quality control, and shipping.

Note that if direct labor cost was the primary concern, the departments would focus on entirely different objectives. Some of this effort would conflict with what was best for the company — short lead times for its customers. Trying to decrease labor costs would surely result in creating backlogs to keep everyone busy. This would increase waiting time

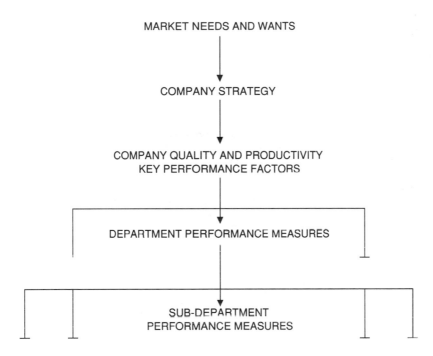

Figure 4.1 Performance Measures Must Reflect Company Strategy

throughout the entire production system. Not only that, but administrative, sales, and manufacturing support departments would probably not even be considered in the overall plan to improve company performance.

Since it is not possible to maximize all variables at the same time, "performance" must usually be defined as maximizing or minimizing a few variables while operating within given constraints. For example, the objectives of a materials management department might be stated as:

> Minimize total cost (unit cost plus inventory cost) while maintaining a service level of 97.5 percent and buying products which meet established standards from approved vendors.

This is quite different from saying, "Get the lowest prices, don't have any stockouts, and minimize inventory."

COMPANY
    Order cycle time
    Service level; on-time delivery
    Quality level (returns, complaints)
    Profit margin

SALES/ORDER ENTRY
    Percent of orders with standard lead time
    Percent of orders with less than normal lead time
    Order processing time to production release

ENGINEERING
    Time to release drawings
    Number of changes to specifications
    Number of drawing errors
    Reworks and delay time attributable to Engineering

MATERIALS MANAGEMENT
    Percent of purchased parts delivered on time
    Production delays attributable to Purchasing
    Quality problems attributable to purchased parts
    Inventory levels

MANUFACTURING
    Percent on-time shipments (normal orders)
    Percent on-time shipments (rush orders)
    Manufacturing time (from drawing release)
    Quality problems attributable to Manufacturing

Figure 4.2 Company and Department Key Performance
Factors Assuming Short Order Cycle Times
Provide a Competitive Advantage

Figure 4.3 shows how "performance" might be defined for some common business functions. In practice, it may be difficult to know exactly what figure should be put on a constraint factor. In that case, make your best guess. As you develop some performance history and experience, you will be able to make a better judgment and revise the constraint factor later. Also, as performance improves, the definition of acceptable levels should be revised accordingly.

MAINTENANCE
> Minimize production time lost because of maintenance problems
> Minimize waste caused by machine problems
> Machine performance must meet production specifications

CUSTOMER SERVICE
> 95% of phone calls picked up within 30 seconds
> 90% of letters/calls answered within 1 day of receipt
> 100% of letters/calls answered within 1 week of receipt
> Minimize inquiries requiring 2 or more contacts to be resolved

EMPLOYEE BENEFITS ADMINISTRATION
> 95% of claims and inquiries processed within 1 week of submittal
> 100% of regulatory filings completed on time
> Minimize employee complaints as percent of claims processed

ENGINEERING
> Design cycle time less than 4 weeks from receipt of specifications
> Minimize revisions per drawing after release
> Customer satisfaction measured by follow-up inquiry 6 months after delivery

Figure 4.3 Definition of "Performance" for Selected Departments

Defining compatible performance measures can have a positive impact on performance in two ways. First, resources committed to non-productive tasks become available for activities that really count. Second, by getting everyone moving in the same direction, waste caused by conflicts and confusion is reduced. Confusion alone can reduce productivity several percentage points.

We've all heard stories of companies that decide to get "lean and mean" and find out they can still function quite well, if not better, with 20 percent less overhead fat. Why have they been overweight for years? Most likely because they lost sight of what really was important for their business. They probably also made the mistake of confusing activity with productivity.

If you recently haven't taken a good hard look at what everyone is doing in your company or department, it's a good bet that as much as 20 percent of the work is useless.[27] For example, when times were tough, Houston Lighting & Power Company went through an extensive analysis of what they were doing. They found they could reduce employment from 11,600 to 10,400 employees *and* create a sorely needed 150-person marketing department that cost nothing to create.[28] If a football coach told his team, "Get out there and win, but two of you guys are going to run a different play when the ball is snapped," he wouldn't last long in any league. But many companies are doing exactly that. It's tough to win with that kind of handicap.

Summary

Maximizing the total productivity of a business is a delicate balancing act that must be accomplished by management. Maximum performance can only be achieved if a department has specific performance measures that reflect the company's key performance factors. Taking the easy way out by asking for everything will not work. It will create conflicts, cause confusion, waste resources, and lower morale. It is simply impossible to maximize everything.

Greed may pay in some circumstances, but not when trying to improve performance. This isn't news. Aesop warned about being greedy in 600 B.C. in his fable about the dog who lost his bone when he tried to grab the second one he saw reflected in a pond. That lesson still applies today.

With apologies to George Orwell, let it be said that:

> *All measures of performance are important,*
> *but some are more important than others.*

Understanding what matters most for a company and its functional parts is the first step to improving performance. Without a clear sense of purpose and consistent objectives throughout a company, it will never come close to realizing its full potential.

CHAPTER 5

Measuring the Performance
of a Production Process

What Needs to Be Measured

Identifying key performance factors is important, but that alone will not give managers the information they need to improve performance. Figure 5.1 shows the variables that must be measured to properly monitor a production process, whether it is a department, a person, or a physical process:

- *Resource inputs* are the money, manpower, and materials used to produce the products.
- *Work inputs* are the demands made on the production system. Orders to fill and the number of letters to be typed are work inputs.
- *Environmental factors* are forces or conditions outside the production system which affect its performance. Procurement lead time for materials and the unemployment rate are examples.
- *Quality inputs* are measures of the quality of incoming work. This could include measurements taken on incoming parts or raw material to determine if it is meeting specifications.
- *Operational variance inputs* (called "variances" after this) are unrecognized quality problems generally not

directly associated with the product. They are any deviation from ideal conditions from the customer's viewpoint in any phase of a production process. Illegible numbers on orders and missing dimensions on a drawing are examples. Variances are discussed in more detail later.

- *Product outputs* are the useful products or services produced. Pounds of yarn and telephone calls made are product outputs.
- *Productivity* is the ratio of output to input as discussed earlier. There could be several productivity measures of interest in a situation. Trying to combine all measures of productivity into one number isn't worth the effort. Besides, there is no generally accepted way to do it.
- *Waste* is present in most processes. Although we usually think of waste in terms of material, it is any resource that does not result in useful output. Measuring waste helps account for the gap between theoretical and actual productivity. Most companies are wallowing in waste and don't know it.
- *Quality outputs* measure how well the goods or services produced conform to their specifications.
- *Variance outputs* are a special type of quality measure as discussed above.
- *Performance, behavior, and diagnostic measures* are not precise terms because the label put on a variable depends on the point of reference. However, it is helpful to distinguish them as follows. Performance measures are the top level gauges of how well the production system is operating in a good/bad sense. Behavior measures are the second level factors that explain how the major parts of the production system interact. Diagnostic measures are used to isolate problems to their actionable level.

These are neat definitions, but in the real world, a given measure could be wearing all these labels at the same time. The point isn't to put every measure in one class or another, but to think of these purposes when deciding what must be measured.

- *Constraints* are variables that must be held within certain limits. They can be real, like capacity limits, or conceptual, such as a maximum order processing time. In any case, constraint factors must be measured to assure they are not violated.

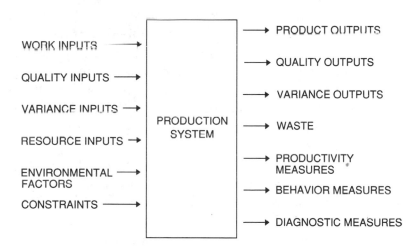

Figure 5.1 Measurements Required to Monitor the Performance of any Production System

The model represents a production system such as a person or department. In a real situation, there would be many production systems forming larger systems. Each one would have its own set of performance measures. Some of these measures will overlap. A performance measure for a subsystem might be a diagnostic measure for its parent, for instance.

Figure 5.2 lists some business functions and performance measures that might apply to them.

In a typical business, there might be several major departments, each needing anywhere from ten to fifty measurements not including the normal accounting functions. This may seem like a large number of variables to measure, but it is not costly to monitor that many parameters with a well-designed system. Precise formulas cannot be established for how many variables have to be measured because every situation is different. However, experience indicates that something in the order of ten to thirty variables is usually sufficient for a department. Figure 5.3 lists the variables that might be appropriate for measuring a customer service department.

The key to having a cost-effective performance measurement system is to measure everything that matters and not much else. It is costly to collect, store, and process data. If the right data is collected and converted to *useful* information which results in decisions and actions, the savings will exceed the costs by a wide margin.

However, like everything that works well, an effective performance measurement system is the result of good initial design and then development through trial and error. Some ideas that look good on paper won't work very well in practice. Typically, more detail is required than first imagined and data collection forms need a few adjustments to make them easy to use. With a little effort, a great deal of data can be collected very efficiently at minimal cost by spreading the task over the entire organization.

One point to note about the model is that it implies the performance of any business function can be measured by one means or another. The model makes no distinction between line and staff functions. Time frames, methods, and variables may change, but the performance of any production system can be measured to a useful degree. Even intangible

	ENGINEERING	PURCHASING	MACHINING	ORDER ENTRY
RESOURCE INPUTS	labor hours labor costs total departmental costs	labor hours labor costs total departmental costs	labor hours maintenance costs material costs	labor hours total departmental costs
WORK INPUTS	product changes new products	requisitions change orders	work orders	orders received order changes
VARIANCE INPUTS	specification errors specification changes	requisition errors change orders	raw material defects drawing errors	errors/omissions order changes
ENVIRONMENTAL INPUTS	sales forecast	delivery lead time	work backlog	sales forecast
WORK OUTPUTS	drawing changes new drawings	purchase orders RFPs cost savings	units produced	orders entered backorders entered
WASTE MEASURES	redesign time	rejected $ units	rework time rejects	idle time shipment errors
VARIANCE OUTPUTS	drawing errors delayed drawing release	purchase order errors late material	defective parts quantity errors	errors entry delays
PRODUCTIVITY	drawing release time hours/change order $ cost / $ sales	cost/order $ saved / $ cost	units / labor hour	orders/labor hour $ cost / $ sales
QUALITY	on-time release drawing errors	late deliveries $ rejects / $ purchases	rejects dimension variance	errors processing time

Figure 5.2 Business Functions and Some Possible Performance Measures

WORK INPUTS

Orders received*
Line items ordered
Inquiries received
 Product availability
 Pricing
 Returns
 Use of product
Complaints received
 Minor (by product, reason)
 Major (by product, reason)

QUALITY INPUTS

Illegible orders
Confused customers

ENVIRONMENTAL FACTORS

Computer system down time
Late mail delivery
Phone system down time/problems

PRODUCTIVITY

Standard orders processed/hour
Standard order processing cost
Inquiries processed/hour
Inquiry processing cost
Complaints processed/hour
Complaint processing cost

WORK OUTPUTS

Orders processed
Line items processed
Inquiries processed
 Product availability
 Pricing
 Returns
 Use of product
Complaints processed
 Minor (by product, reason)
 Major (by product, reason)
 Corrective action
  Refund
  Replacement
  Special

QUALITY OUTPUTS

Orders not entered within 24 hours
Order entry errors
% inquiries processed on first call,
 two or more calls
% inquiries not answered in 24 hours
% complaints not resolved in 24 hours
% complaints not resolved by department
Customer satisfaction index
 (from reply card enclosed with order)

* Work would come in by telephone and letter. Although it would be important to know the mix, for simplicity, this distinction is not made in the list. It also would be important to know the distribution of incoming work by day and even by hour.

Figure 5.3 Performance Measures for a Customer Service Department

factors like morale, attitudes, and customer satisfaction can be measured.[29]

Of course, trying to measure the performance of a production system which only consumes resources and produces no useful output is an exercise in futility. For this reason, the model does not apply to many federal government agencies.

"Measured" does not necessarily mean direct measurement in absolute terms such as feet or pounds. A variable may also be measured indirectly by measuring its effect on something else. Low morale, for example, may be indicated by an increase in turnover and absenteeism. In this case, the measure is not absolute, but relative. Even though no universally recognized "morale index" exists, it is still possible to look at historical data and get a better understanding of which way and how fast you are changing.

Not just any number is a useful number. Performance measures must be carefully selected and validated by checking them against reality. Good performance measurement systems are developed, not designed. A "good" system is one which provides a manager with timely, reliable information which is relevant to the decisions he or she has to make. If an information system doesn't meet this test, it is isn't worth much no matter how sophisticated it may be.

Measuring a Production System: An Example

To illustrate how a production system might be measured, let's consider the "Table Setting Production System" shown by Figure 5.4. The flowchart shows the important steps in the process, with the end product being a clean set table for the next customer. The process consists of three distinct phases, with one person responsible for each phase (although the number of people is irrelevant).

How would the performance of this production system be measured? Let's start with the busboy. The basic work input

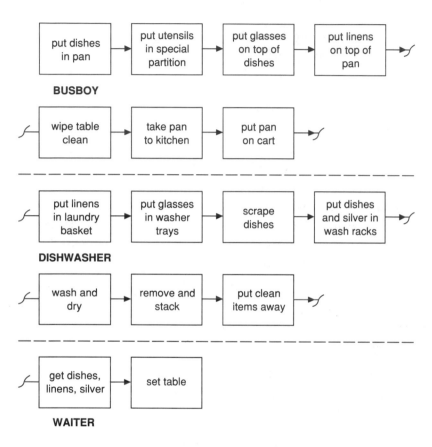

Figure 5.4 Table Setting Production System

he receives is the number of tables he has to clear. But that doesn't give a true picture of the workload. There is a difference between tables with one person and those with six, so we also need to measure the number of places served. Similarly, the work output would also be measured by the number of tables and places cleaned.

What are some quality and variance problems the busboy might have to face? Spills and plates broken by falling on the floor come to mind. Another likely variance is Really Cruddy Messes (RCMs), the natural result of two or more children under six years old who think food is an art form.

The quality of the busboy's work would be measured by observing if the table was clean (recorded by the waiter) and by chipped or broken items. Note that if we are going to know where breakage is taking place, it will have to be measured at each phase of the process. Only knowing broken dishes are increasing will not be sufficient to isolate the problem so something can be done about it.

Broken items are also a waste factor. Another form of waste is "lost eat time," the time lost because the busboy and/or waiter are slow in clearing and setting the table.

The variables that should be measured to know how the system is performing are shown by Figure 5.5. Take the time to review the performance measures and relate it to the flowchart.

Collecting the data would not be difficult. The number of tables and places can be obtained from the bills which also could provide a place to indicate complaints or compliments. Broken or chipped items need to be thrown away, and could be separated and tabulated as they are found. The same goes for dirty dishes or utensils. Counting buspans, plate racks, and glass racks is easy.

About the only variable that might be difficult to measure is "lost eat time," which is the time lost when a customer is waiting for a table to be cleared and set. One possible method is simply for the waiter to note the number of times he had to wait longer than normal for a table to be cleaned. This wouldn't give a direct measure of the lost minutes, but it would provide a relative index which would indicate when delays were getting excessive. Another possibility is for the hostess to make an estimate since she would know when customers were waiting and tables should be available.

WORK INPUTS	QUALITY/ VARIANCE INPUTS	WORK OUTPUT	QUALITY OUTPUT	WASTE	ENVIRON- MENTAL	PRODUCTIVITY
BUSBOY						
# tables # places	broken items spills RCMs* special seating	tables cleaned places cleaned	chipped dishes table cleanliness	broken items lost eat time	patrons served	places/hr
DISHWASHER						
# buspans # plate racks # glass racks	mixed up pans	# wash racks	dirty silver dirty plates dirty glasses	idle hours downtime hours broken items	utility outage	wash racks/hr
WAITER						
tables to set places to set	broken items dirty items dirty tables	tables set places set	dirty items complaints	lost eat time	special seating	places/hr

* Really Cruddy Messes

Figure 5.5 *Performance Measures for the Table Setting Production System*

These performance measures would give the manager a good picture of the restaurant's performance from an operational viewpoint. If the manager paid attention to the numbers and actual events, after a few months he would know that "normal" performance looked like and what staffing would be required for anticipated business. For example, if "lost eat time" and complaints were increasing at certain peak times, it might pay to have additional help at those times.

A daily summary report would help explain any unusual performance. Plotting the weekly (and possibly daily) figures on a graph would show trends. As performance history was developed, it would be possible to estimate the normal range of each variable, enabling exceptions to be identified.

This example is not presented to suggest this is the way to manage a restaurant, but to show how the production system could be measured. As this example illustrates, in many respects there really isn't much difference between measuring a restaurant's performance and the factory that makes its plates.

Operational Requirements for an Effective Performance Measurement System

Measuring all the right variables in a production system is the first condition for an effective performance measurement system, but it is not enough. To be effective, it will also have to meet the following requirements.

Validity

The performance measures must be valid. That is, they must measure what counts and be accepted and understood by the users. A manufacturing vice president confided:

> "We have this system that we use to award bonuses, but it's a big joke. It is supposed to measure performance, but it doesn't and everybody knows it. I don't know why we persist in using it."

Why indeed? If anything, it lowers morale, increases costs, and makes management look foolish. Better to admit the system doesn't work and change it, than to continue living in a dream world.

If those affected by the performance measures do not believe they are valid, then they either don't understand the system or it is not correct. The problems need to be identified and resolved. They cannot be allowed to persist, or the system is a waste of time and money.

Completeness

The productivity and quality measures must be designed to prevent people from doing the wrong things as much as it will guide them to do the right things. It must be "closed" in the sense that it considers *all* aspects of the balancing act that have to be performed. For example, do not measure productivity and ignore customer service or product quality. The "box" that the person or department must stay within must have all the important sides in place to guide behavior in the right direction.

Sufficient Detail

In information theory, there is a concept known as *variety*. It can be thought of as the number of different ways something can respond. As a system's variety increases, more information is needed to describe its behavior. For example, a light bulb's behavior can be explained with two words, "on" and "off." To describe the status of three bulbs, eight different combinations of "on" and "off" are needed, and so forth. Another illustration is the difference in variety between chess and checkers. There are more movement options in chess, so there is more variety in the game.

Associated with the concept of variety is a principle known as the Law of Requisite Variety. It states that if a system is to be controlled, the controlling system must have at least as much variety as the system to be controlled. In other words, *complex systems cannot be controlled by simple mechanisms.*

For example, imagine a football team with only two offensive plays competing against a team using several hundred options. Which team would you bet on to win? You might also imagine trying to fly a modern airplane using the same control systems the Wright Brothers used. You probably wouldn't fly much further than they did before you crashed.

Businesses are complex systems. What the Law of Requisite Variety means is that if you are going to control and improve the performance of your business, it will be necessary to control many variables. This cannot be done with a simple information system. You will need to know what is happening at the actionable levels of each production system in the company.

An example of how the lack of detail can be misleading was a company experiencing cash flow problems. Of all the potential causes, the CEO felt that inventory control was not a problem because the turnover ratio was good by industry standards. However, analysis of the individual products revealed they were in two groups: (1) those that were never in stock and (2) those that had several years supply in stock. Clearly, inventory control was a problem, but it couldn't be seen by looking at the summary information.

Similar situations are likely to be found anywhere. The average appears acceptable, but beneath the surface, there are many problems and opportunities waiting to be discovered. This is the natural result of combining the activities of different groups. As shown by Figure 5.6, as individual performance information is combined, the amount of variation that can be seen decreases. You can demonstrate this principle yourself by flipping a coin and keeping track of the ratio of heads to tails. The more tries you record, the closer the ratio will get to one.

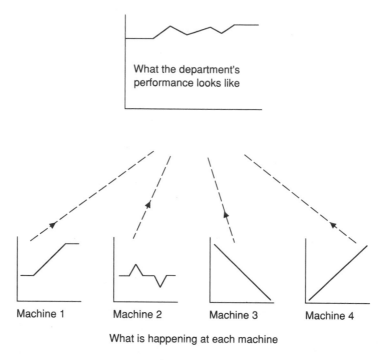

Machine 1   Machine 2   Machine 3   Machine 4

What is happening at each machine

Figure 5.6 Combining Information Reduces Visible Variation

This principle explains why the people doing the work can contribute so much to improving performance. They see problems and know details of their job that are completely unknown to an outsider.

It also explains why top-down planning and decision-making is most effective when it is supplemented by bottom-up information. The Japanese approach of getting everyone involved in planning may take longer than the typical U.S. approach, but implementation is rapid because everyone knows their role and many potential stumbling blocks can be avoided. Taking advantage of inside information is illegal when you're trading stocks, but not when you're managing a department or a business.

Since only specific problems can be solved, *the only place where something positive can be done about productivity or quality is at the actionable level — the source of the problem or where the activity takes place.* Referring to Figure 5.7, the problem can be corrected only if we know the problem is the result of causes A3, B2 and C1. If all we know is that the department's performance is slipping, we only have an indication of a problem — a symptom. We can ask the department head to explain what is going on, but unless he has detailed performance information about each machine, he won't be able to give a definite answer. He will probably mumble something like: "Just a bad week — we'll do much better this week." And he will probably do that by compensating for the problem until the "exception" occurs again.

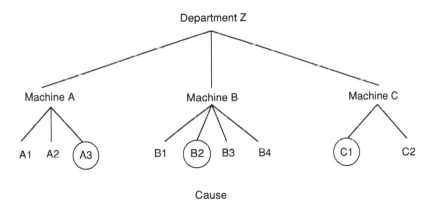

If Department Z's performance is decreasing, it is only a symptom of a problem. Unless the reason for poor performance can be isolated to specific causes on specific machines, the problem will not be corrected. It may be possible to compensate for the problem, but at best that can only provide some temporary relief.

Figure 5.7 Problems Must Be Isolated to the Actionable Level Before They Can Be Solved

Figure 5.8 is another illustration of the need for detailed information. The diagram could represent an electronic circuit, a mechanical system, or a production system. Assume it is an electronic circuit and the output isn't correct. If all we can measure is the input and output, all we know is that something is wrong somewhere between the two points. One or more of the modules is defective, but without being able to measure between the modules, all we can do is exchange modules until we hit the right combination. Business problems are no different: without visibility all the way down to the actionable level, more expensive guesswork is required.

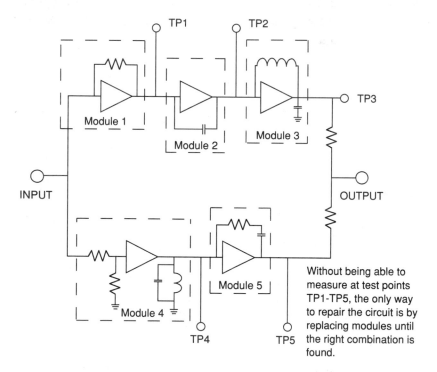

Figure 5.8 If Only the Output of a System Is Measured, the Problems within It Cannot Be Isolated

Lack of detail hinders identifying, diagnosing, and solving problems. Many managers simply don't get the performance information they need to make good decisions. As one sales manager complained:

> "All I get is month-to-date and year-to-date figures that are three to six weeks late. I never get the detail I need to understand what's going on in the market and what my salesmen are doing."

He speaks for many of his peers. The answer, however, is not to throw paper at the problem by churning out detailed listings of every sales transaction. Instead, the data must be converted into a form which satisfies his specific needs.

Accounting for the Performance Gap

The measurement system must account for at least 80 percent of the gap (or variation) between actual and desired or normal performance. For example, if machine downtime was being measured, the total of the individual causes should add up to at least 80 percent of non-operating time as illustrated by Figure 5.9. In practice, getting to 90 or 95 percent is normally possible.

Why is accounting for the gap important? Because if you can't explain the gap, you haven't identified all the significant causes of the variations in the output of the production system. If you haven't done that, you really don't know what's happening. Generally speaking, 20 percent of the causes will account for 80 percent or more of the variation in output. The others will be so small, they don't need to be measured — at least until performance improves to the point where they become significant.

Sufficient Measurement Frequency

As Figure 5.10A illustrates, if measurements are not taken often enough, a distorted picture results. Increasing

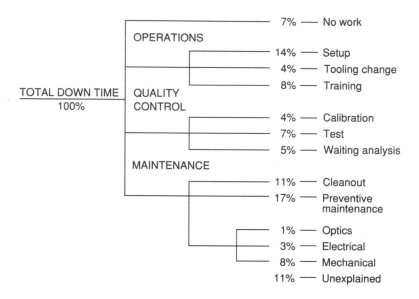

*Figure 5.9 A Good Performance Measurement System Must Explain
at least 80% of the Performance Gap*

the sampling frequency presents a truer picture. The measurement frequency must be consistent with the response time of the system. Six to eight samples during the period a variable can change significantly is sufficient. A variable that can change considerably during a week should be measured daily. If it can change substantially during a day, it should be measured every hour.

There is no advantage to measuring more frequently than needed; it only increases costs. Usually, daily reporting and graphing weekly performance is sufficient. This excludes, of course, physical processes and other areas where large changes can happen in a few minutes. In those cases, more frequent measurements and more precise measures are needed.

Another important aspect of measurement frequency is that problems rarely stay solved forever. They must be continually

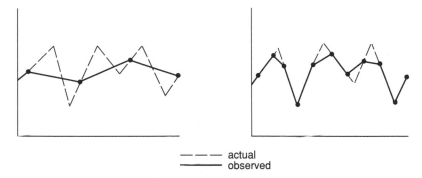

Figure 5.10A *If the Sampling Frequency Is too Low, the Information Can Be Misleading*

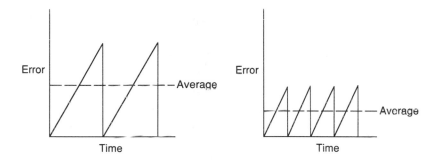

Figure 5.10B *Increasing the Frequency of Measurement and Action Decreases the Average Level of a Problem*

beaten back into submission. In any production system, new problems will develop and old ones will resurface for any number of reasons. Taking corrective action more frequently decreases the average level of a problem. This is illustrated by Figure 5.10B.

Timeliness

Having the right information is one thing; having it when you need it is quite another. Time lag is important because too much delay between a stimulus and the corresponding response makes learning difficult. Try learning to play tennis by watching tapes of yesterday's practice session!

Timeliness is also essential for diagnosing problems. Memories are short, especially in business where there are so many events happening each day. Right now, try writing down what happened to you three days ago. Difficult? If you're like most people, it won't be easy, even if you refer to your daily calendar.

Information loses its value very quickly in business, particularly when you are trying to investigate a problem. Office gossip will be remembered forever, but if a few days have passed, recalling important details about problems is nearly impossible, even when someone tries their best. If a person is in the small minority that wants to cover their tracks, a few days delay provides plenty of time to do it.

A good rule of thumb is that a manager needs to have a complete picture of what happened *yesterday*. In some cases, that might be too late. It is difficult to think of a situation where being behind more than a day or two would be acceptable. There is a big difference between knowing *what is happening* and *what happened*. Considering the inexpensive tools available today for processing data, there is no excuse for any manager or supervisor not to be completely informed about his department's performance on a timely basis.

Richard P. Simmons, CEO of Allegheny Ludlum Steel attributes much of his company's success to having timely detailed information on all aspects of the business available to his managers. "If you give good people good data, on a timely basis, good people will do good things," Mr. Simmons says, explaining his creed. It is a basic, he believes, that much of American industry has lost sight of — or ignored — in its infatuation with fads, quick fixes, and growth-by-acquisition.[30]

The value of timely information is well understood in Japan. There, it is common practice to place warning lights at work stations so when problems arise, they can be diagnosed when they are happening. Contrast this with a company try-ing to solve its quality problems by saving all the rejects until the end of the week, and then reviewing them in a group meeting. The result? According to the manufacturing VP, fin-ger-pointing, buck-passing, and foot-shuffling. Everything but problem-solving. Agreement is rarely reached on the cause of a problem, let alone a solution. With the long time delay between when the problem occurred and when action was taken to identify the cause, little else could happen.

Managers would do well to learn what every hound dog knows by instinct — it's easier to follow a hot trail than a cold one.

Useful Accuracy

Highly accurate figures are generally not required for per-formance information to be useful. *In most cases, what we need to know for identifying problems and guiding behavior is not the ab-solute value of a performance measure, but whether or not its trend is up or down and how its current value compares with historical performance.*

If the data collection method is consistent, the error in the data will tend to be consistent, minimizing the error in the difference between measurements taken at different times. For example, although the real number of errors is important, for the purpose of improving performance, we don't really care whether errors have gone from 8 percent to 6 percent or from 6.5 percent to 4.5 percent. What is important is that we know the steps taken reduced errors by 2 percent.

Accuracy is a relative term. High-precision manufacturing processes obviously require high-precision measurements. It's nice to be as accurate as possible, but it is not necessary to use a micrometer to measure firewood. The trend is what matters most for guiding behavior and making decisions. Being consistent and reasonably accurate is all that is needed to have useful performance information.

Long-term Consistency

The measurement units must not be affected by changes in product mix, production volumes, or other factors that may change with time. This will make historical comparisons possible. Percentages or ratios are usually best.

It may be necessary to use the most common item of production as a "standard unit" and convert other outputs to that base. For example, a furniture manufacturer making sofas, chairs, and loveseats might use a popular chair as a standard and convert all units produced to that base. That way, if the product mix changes over time, historical comparisons can still be made.

Here again, absolute accuracy is not required. Good estimates of the number of "equivalent chairs" in a particular type of sofa will be sufficient. Small errors will wash out over a period of a week or month, making the percentage error in total units produced even smaller.

Striving for long-term consistency should not override making changes in measures to accommodate changes in products or the production process, but knowing where you came from can be important. Careful consideration of the units of measure and keeping a record of adjustments will make long term comparisons possible.

Easily Understood Terms

The measures used must be easily understood by the people using them. It is easier for most people to relate to things they work with every day like pounds of waste, invoicing errors, or percentage of screws rejected. Talking about "percentage variance to standard cost budget" may mean something to the accounting department (although it might not) but it isn't likely to get much attention from anyone else.

Translating quality or production problems into costs, lost wages, or benefits can help people appreciate the cost of poor performance, but it is better to use familiar terms for day-to-day communications.

If you want people to understand what you are saying,
speak in their language, not yours.

Accountability

While accountability is not a property of a performance measurement system, the system will not be of much value unless there is strict accountability for each and every measure. This means that one, and only one person is assigned the responsibility for each measure. That person should be the one who is most directly responsible for the variable or who has the largest share of the problem.

In the case of the inventory manager discussed earlier, if someone in the plant was not filling out a transaction form correctly, he couldn't get away with just pointing his finger at someone else. It was his responsibility to see the person received instruction or a reprimand by going through proper channels.

Holding one person accountable does not prevent the use of cross-functional teams, Quality Circles, or other programs. In fact, it makes such activities more productive by improving communications, preventing problems from falling through the cracks, speeding up decision-making, and focusing resources on the right priorities.

If more than one person is held accountable for anything,
no one is accountable.

Trust and Credibility

The output of an information system can be no better than its input. If the people in an organization do not trust each other, then the data reported and the information exchanged will be filtered or distorted. This can be done subconsciously or deliberately and is difficult to detect. Whether it is by commission or omission, when incorrect information reaches management, bad decisions will be made.

Managers must strive to maintain an environment where people feel free to report mistakes, admit problems, have differences of opinion, and exchange ideas. In an atmosphere of fear and distrust, the distortion and filtering of information makes improving performance very difficult.

The Shortcomings of Accounting Systems

Accounting systems provide a great deal of necessary and useful information, but as a tool for improving performance, they have serious shortcomings. To identify the shortcomings, let's see how accounting systems satisfy the requirements for an effective performance measurement system.

Validity

Although accountants can get very creative at times, accounting reports generally present a fair picture from a score-keeping perspective.

Completeness

Other than sales and units manufactured, accounting systems measure resources consumed much better than they measure the useful outputs to be produced. Performance measures other than budget variances are generally missing, which can encourage the wrong kind of behavior. For example, in one company, managers were spending much more time debating who was going to get charged for rejects instead of solving the problem.

Accounting systems also view departments as independent entities, which they are not. Relationships between activities are not evident or necessarily even considered. This promotes narrow-minded departmental thinking and suboptimization, instead of cooperative efforts to achieve common higher goals.

Detail

Even though costs may be tracked down to a single person or operation, that point can still be several levels removed from the actionable level. Accounting systems rarely report more than symptoms and they may miss many of those by consolidating data from many sources.

Accounting for the Performance Gap

In accounting terms, performance gaps are explained very well, but the information may not be easily correlated with actual operations. Also, as mentioned earlier, detail may be lacking and many important performance measures are usually missing in the first place.

Frequency

Once a month is not enough. Few accounting systems provide more than gross summary reports on a weekly basis, let alone detailed daily reports.

Timeliness

In business, as in medicine, it is important to try to cure the living. Unfortunately, the delays inherent in accounting systems make most of the information only useful for counting the dead.

Accuracy

Accounting reports are very accurate if you disregard the distortions caused by timing, allocating costs, and "adjustments."

Long-term Consistency

Consistency could be good or bad depending on how well the system accounts for changes in the product mix and whether "per unit" information exists. Inflation and changes in allocation methods can make historical comparisons meaningless unless you can factor in all the footnotes.

Understanding

At the lower levels, accounting figures don't have much meaning. At the higher levels, understanding is usually fair to good, assuming the account structure reflects actual operations. Managers should be telling their accountants how they want their information presented, not the other way around.

Measuring the Right Variables

Dollars are important, but they don't measure quality, on-time deliveries, and hundreds of other factors managers need to know. Dollars keep score, but they provide little information that can be used to improve the score.

The shortcomings of accounting systems are illustrated by the problems encountered in one company when it replaced an entrepreneur's tracking system with a modern standard-cost system. The former CEO reported:

> . . . The trade was a disaster...the prior owner had one of the cleverest monitoring systems I had ever seen. For example, he received a daily report on the percent of virgin versus off-grade material being used in a critical mixing process. This figure kept track of how aggressively the operators were taking advantage of cheaper materials to achieve good final product. It also let him know when the operators had lost control over this large and pivotal process.

> . . . There were more than a dozen other figures that this man tracked on a daily or weekly basis...I can assure you, if his operation missed a beat, the alarm bells went off immediately.

> The new standard-cost system would have been great as a complement to the prior owner's system, but it wasn't even a close substitute. The standard-cost data came out monthly, lacking sensitivity and timeliness.[31]

The purpose of this discussion is not to find fault with accountants or accounting systems, but to point out that accounting systems cannot provide managers with all the information they need to effectively manage performance. Although even some accountants feel current accounting practices need drastic overhaul[32], *the basic problem is that accounting systems are not designed to manage operations, but to report the financial results of that management.* That is a very important difference.

As this case indicates, in most business functions there are a few key variables which are the pulse of the operation. Keep these under control and profits will naturally follow. In other words, measure and control the process instead of putting all your attention on the result. But you can't keep the variables under control by watching accounting figures. In fact, if you have a good performance measurement system, you will be able to make good projections of financial results long before you get the final figures. As in controlling quality, if you measure and control the process, the results will take care of themselves.

No doubt some managers would like to point fingers at accountants and vice-versa, but that doesn't make the problem go away. The simple fact is that most accounting information is several reporting levels and several weeks removed from the activity that produced the numbers. The problem will be solved when both managers and accountants recognize the value of addressing both needs and then take the necessary steps to fill them. As Skinner put it in reference to manufacturing:

> . . . By now our accounting and control systems are pathetically old-fashioned and ineffective. But nothing changes. Our continuing obsession with productivity as the be-all measure of factory performance is to blame, not the stubbornness of accountants.[33]

Summary

The quality of any decision is limited by the information available when it is made. Managers at all levels need performance information to make good decisions about when and where action is needed. Department managers and supervisors especially need timely performance information about their area of responsibility, since that is most often where something can be done to minimize problems and improve the production process.

Unfortunately, meaningful information at the actionable level is often missing. As a result, management is often blissfully unaware of many problems and potential opportunities. Accounting systems alone cannot fill all of management's needs for information, especially when it comes to improving quality and productivity.

By themselves, accounting systems are not complete management information systems even though that misnomer will probably exist forever. It is more than a question of semantics: by no stretch of the imagination can current accounting systems provide managers with all the information they need to make timely and effective decisions. Accounting systems must be supplemented with systems that measure operational performance.

CHAPTER 6

The Simple Truth About Statistical Process Control

The Control Process

Controlling any variable consists of first determining the difference between its current value and what it should be. Then, steps are taken to reduce the difference to as close to zero as possible. This is how a guidance system keeps a missile on course. When the missile tilts, a gyroscope senses the movement and generates an electrical signal proportional to the missile's position. This fires a small rocket engine which moves the missile back to the correct position, at which point the error signal is zero.

Unless you're a taxi driver in New York City, this is the same way you drive a car. Your eyes sense where you are on the road and you reduce the difference between where you are and where you want to be to zero by turning the steering wheel.

If you want to control quality, the process is the same. As shown by Figure 6.1, you need to:

1. Define a specification for the product or process — what it should "look like."
2. Next you need to measure the specified properties of the product and compare them to the specification.

At this point, you can "control" quality by rejecting any product not meeting the specification. This will assure that quality standards are met, but it does nothing to improve the production process. If you want to improve quality, additional steps are required. The most efficient way to do it is to:

3. Identify what is causing the output of the production system to deviate from the desired level.
4. Devise a change to the system which you think will improve its performance.
5. Implement the proposed solution.
6. Measure the output to see if the changes made actually improved the system's performance.
7. If the expected results were achieved, concentrate on the next problem. If the output did not improve, you either didn't understand the causes of the problem or your solution was ineffective. Give yourself credit for trying, take advantage of what you learned, and try something else.

This is a straightforward procedure. It is simply an application of the Scientific Method, which has existed for at least several centuries as a formal discipline. It is the basis for controlling and improving any performance measure. For the process to work, we must know the difference between where we are and where we want to be. If this gap can't be measured, good control is nearly impossible and it is difficult even to verify that implemented "solutions" actually improved performance.

Capability

No matter how simple or complex a production system may be, when its output is measured we will observe it has two important qualities:

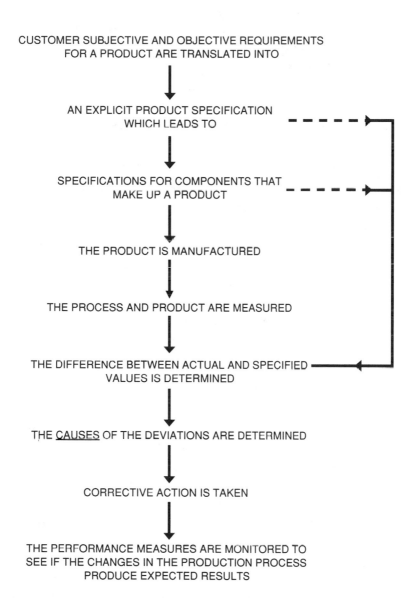

CUSTOMER SUBJECTIVE AND OBJECTIVE REQUIREMENTS
FOR A PRODUCT ARE TRANSLATED INTO

AN EXPLICIT PRODUCT SPECIFICATION
WHICH LEADS TO

SPECIFICATIONS FOR COMPONENTS THAT
MAKE UP A PRODUCT

THE PRODUCT IS MANUFACTURED

THE PROCESS AND PRODUCT ARE MEASURED

THE DIFFERENCE BETWEEN ACTUAL AND SPECIFIED
VALUES IS DETERMINED

THE CAUSES OF THE DEVIATIONS ARE DETERMINED

CORRECTIVE ACTION IS TAKEN

THE PERFORMANCE MEASURES ARE MONITORED TO
SEE IF THE CHANGES IN THE PRODUCTION PROCESS
PRODUCE EXPECTED RESULTS

Figure 6.1 The Quality Control Process

- The output will always have some degree of variation caused by factors that are an inherent part of the process.
- If the system is operating normally, the output will stay within specific limits. This operating range defines the system's *capability* — what it can do and how well it can do it.

Every production system has a capability. People, racehorses, machines, and organizations all have a limited capability which, by definition, cannot be exceeded. Trying to make a machine operate beyond its design limits will destroy it or greatly shorten its life.

People aren't much different. You might get a short burst of peak performance from a person or group, but no amount of "motivation" is going to change someone's fundamental abilities for very long. Expecting any production system to exceed its capability is wishful thinking. As my grandfather used to say:

No matter how hard you rub,
you can't polish horse manure.

It follows that if a production system is going to be managed and used effectively, its capability must be understood. The only way to determine a system's capability is to measure its performance, whether it is a simple machine or a department. Managing a business function or a physical process without knowing its capability is equivalent to selecting a football team from a pool of players without knowing their performance records. You might guess correctly but the odds are against it.

Once the capability of a system or process is determined, it can be compared to what it is expected to do — the specification for the products it is to produce. *If a process is not capable of meeting specifications when it is operating normally, the process must be changed in some manner to improve its capability.* The only other choice is to produce defective products.

On the other hand, if the process is capable of meeting specifications when it is operating properly, all that must be done to produce good products is to keep it running as it should. "Normal operation" can be determined by measuring the system's performance and observing if its future performance is predictable from its past performance. If that is the case, it is said to be "in control" or "stabilized" and its performance will stay between specific limits. Once these limits are known, performance outside the limits indicates something has gone wrong somewhere in the process.

In terms of meeting its requirements, any production system has only the following possibilities:

1. *It has the capability and is in control.* No action is required. The variation in the output is within normal limits and caused by factors inherent in the process — what are often called "common causes" of variation. This is illustrated by Figure 6.2A. Bear in mind, however, that "common" causes are not necessarily permanent causes. They are part of the system in its present form, which can be changed.

2. *It has the capability but is out of control.* Something out of the ordinary (a "special cause") has happened to change the system's behavior. Either the input has changed or something has changed within the process. Corrective action is required to restore the system to its normal operating condition, but correcting the problem will not improve its capability. This is illustrated by Figure 6.2B.

3. *It does not have the capability to meet specifications all the time.* Some products will be good and some will be bad regardless of whether the system is in control or

not. This is illustrated by Figure 6.2C. Of course, the situation is worse if the process is also out of control, but that is a moot point. The process must be improved so it can satisfy its customers' requirements. In effect, some of the common causes must be removed, although that may not be exactly what happens. For example, instead of modifying a machine to improve its capability, a new one may be purchased which is considerably better.

Controlling and Improving Quality

Improving quality and controlling quality are obviously closely related, but they are really two different problems. Assuming a production process can meet specifications, controlling quality amounts to knowing whether it is operating normally or not and correcting problems as they occur.

If a process is in control, improving the quality of its output can only be accomplished by improving its capability. This requires understanding how the process works, the causes of variation in the output, and the factors that limit performance.

Another crucial difference between controlling and improving quality is that *although an operator can control quality, he or she usually can't do much to improve it.* An individual can monitor the output of a process, recognize when something is going wrong and halt the process or take corrective action. However, that person is seldom in a position to make significant changes to the process.

On the other hand, *improving quality by improving capability is primarily management's responsibility since that usually involves the use of resources beyond an individual's control.* It is true that everyone can contribute to improving quality — especially by contributing ideas — but if management doesn't

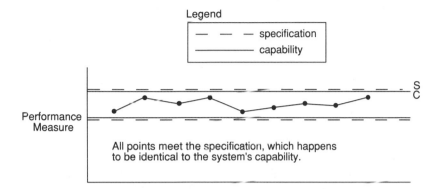

Figure 6.2A *Behavior of a System with Adequate Capability and in Control*

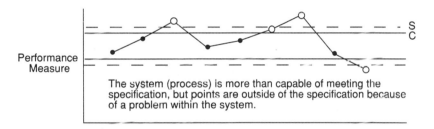

Figure 6.2B *Behavior of a System with Adequate Capability and Out of Control*

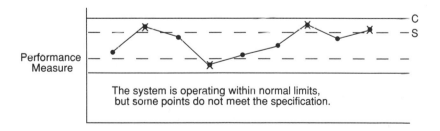

Figure 6.2C *Behavior of a System without Adequate Capability and in Control*

want to change anything or commit resources to the task, not much will happen.

It follows that to make correct decisions about the kind of action required, management must know if quality problems are the result of inadequate capability or special (temporary) problems which can be corrected. The answer to this question is critical because it determines whether the problem belongs to management or the operator. If the process is not capable of producing a product which always meets specifications, it can be "fixed" or adjusted forever without solving the problem. In this situation, blaming employees for a problem they can't correct or tampering with something that isn't broken, will only make matters worse.

There are two primary reasons for measuring performance in general and Statistical Process Control in particular: (1) *to understand the capability of a production process* and (2) *to measure the performance of the process so you know when and what kind of action is required.* The consensus of experts is that the vast majority of quality problems are caused by inherently weak production systems. In other words, most quality and productivity problems are management's responsibility, not the workers'.

Measuring the Process

Quality can be controlled by measuring only the output of a process, but there is a better way to do it. Since quality problems usually have several causes, by measuring each of the *causes* it is usually possible to detect when something is going wrong with the process and correct it *before* defective products are actually produced. In other words, measure and control the process, not just its output.

Oil pressure and engine temperature gauges on a car are simple examples of measuring a production process instead of just the output. They don't guarantee the engine is working properly, but they will indicate critical problems before the engine self-destructs.

In practice, the product as well as the process is usually measured to verify compliance with the specification. In the ideal case, this isn't necessary. If the process has sufficient capability and is in control, the product will be within acceptable limits.

It is important to note that being in control only means a production system or process is operating within normal limits based on past performance. It doesn't mean the system's capability meets requirements. It is possible to have every process in control in a company and still be producing poor quality products.

Even if a process is meeting specifications and is in control, it certainly doesn't mean further improvement is not possible or worthwhile. As discussed earlier, it always pays to get better. As a process becomes more consistent and reliable, it not only becomes more efficient, it also enhances the performance of all operations that follow it.

Processing Data

Having established that it is necessary to measure quality in order to control and improve it, we must turn our attention to converting the data generated by a production process into useful information. Since all processes vary to some degree, statistical methods are the most effective way to convert data into information because statistics is the mathematical language of variation. There simply are no better alternatives.

Fortunately, while some statistical methods can only be understood and used by experts, there are some very effective tools most anyone can use. If any of these methods are used, it is correct to say you are doing "statistical process control" (SPC).

The easiest method for generating useful information is to simply plot the data on a graph or what is called a "run chart" in SPC terms. This is one case where a picture is truly worth a thousand words. Some judgment is required, but reasonably good estimates of what is normal behavior and what is not can often be made using only a simple graph.

Figure 6.3 illustrates why. The graph shows daily efficiency of a machine. Can you guess when something went wrong with the machine and when it was corrected? You could make several statistical calculations to conclude the problem started about Period 9 and was fixed at Period 18, or you could reach the same conclusion directly from the graph. Systems of machines and people have characteristic behavior patterns. Once some performance history has been established, it is usually quite evident when changes need attention.

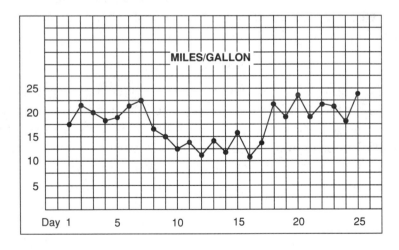

Figure 6.3 Sample Performance Graph

Figure 6.4 is a reproduction of an actual performance graph. As you can see, changes in the process resulted in a steady reduction of defects, with some temporary bumps in the road. You can also see that both the level of rejects and the week-to-week variation in the level decreased. With this information it was possible to conclude that the changes made to the process really did improve performance. Because of the nature of this particular process, once its performance was improved and stabilized it was very evident when something went wrong. In fact, the problems would be noted and the machine would be shut down long before the data could even be processed!

Run charts are the simplest and easiest way to process performance data. The next level of refinement is provided by the basic statistical tools — control charts, histograms, and scatter diagrams. These techniques provide insight into a system's behavior and a degree of sensitivity that cannot be obtained with a run chart. (Pareto charts are often included in this group and will be discussed later.)

Instead of eyeball estimates, control charts (illustrated by Figure 6.2) provide specific numerical limits which can make problems apparent that might be missed on a run chart. Control charts are always necessary for controlling physical processes such as machining parts, applying coatings, high volume production of components, or maintaining close tolerances in any operation.

More advanced statistical techniques may be necessary to understand and control complicated processes. When several variables are interacting to produce an output, statistical analysis may be necessary to identify their individual effect. For example, the surface finish on a sheet of steel might depend on temperature, roller speed, carbon content, and a few other variables. Separating the effect each of those variables

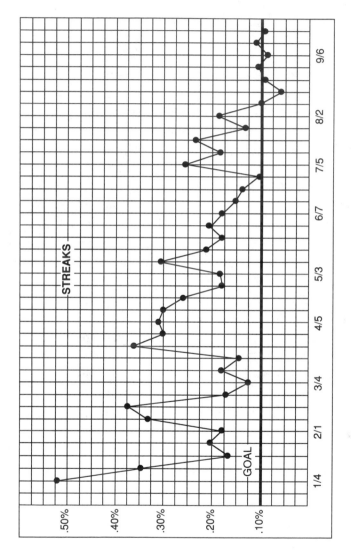

Figure 6.4 Actual Performance Measurement Graph

has on the surface finish may require carefully designed experiments and sophisticated analysis. Only people who are very proficient with statistics should get involved with problems of this nature. Fortunately, most businesses are not faced with many of these very complex problems.

Explaining statistical techniques is not the purpose of this book, so the discussion of them ends here. There are many good books, videotapes, and training courses readily available. The book by Amsden, Butler and Amsden listed under "References" is a good beginner's text.

Statistical analysis is a powerful tool, but the technique used to process the data should be fitted to the task. If you're measuring the right factors, using simple graphs or run charts will let you make considerable progress in most cases. If you're measuring the wrong variables, it doesn't make any difference how you process the data.

Even if more sophisticated techniques are eventually required, simple graphs are a good place to start. Control charts, histograms, scatter diagrams and other techniques can be introduced later after everyone gets used to collecting data and processes are better understood. In any case, control charts are meaningless until a process is stabilized by removing the major causes of poor performance.

Besides, it is better to learn to walk before you try to run. Simple systems understood by everyone are more effective than complicated systems understood by only a select few. For example, in one company that invested heavily in SPC training, I asked a supervisor what use he had made of what he learned. His reply was that although he knew all the technical names for his graphs, he had no idea what they meant or even if he was measuring the right variables!

The objective isn't to generate charts but to understand the performance limits of a process and how it works so management can recognize when and what type of action is required. Then, it is a matter of identifying the causes of poor performance and using the discipline of the Scientific Method to solve temporary problems or improve the capability of the process. If you don't do that, you can crunch numbers until the Devil gets frostbite and you'll never make any progress.

Statistical analysis is not a cure-all. From many articles in the press it is easy to get the impression that all you need to do is start cranking out control charts and all your problems will be solved. As Deming says, however, anyone who expects to achieve productivity and quality through a massive infusion of statistics will be severely disappointed.[34] Although they are essential, the numbers won't tell you if your specifications are correct, that performance can't be improved, what to do to improve performance, that you're measuring the right variables, or that you're working toward the right objectives.

It is important to note that wrong conclusions can be reached from what looks like good data. For example, in a packing department the data on productivity and errors was very consistent. The logical conclusion was that this represented the department's capability. However, a test conducted with a few known people indicated that errors could easily be 50 percent lower and productivity 40 percent higher. When this was tactfully explained to those involved, performance improved dramatically overnight.

Purely physical processes are better behaved than those which involve people, but even with machines, it is always possible for something unusual to happen. In any production system, circumstances may develop where the system's performance is not explained by the variables being measured. Performance information must always be looked at with a little bit of doubt — especially when it doesn't seem consistent with reality. In that case, don't argue with reality, find out what's wrong with the numbers.

No matter what performance information is available, there is no guarantee it is always correct or complete. Managers will still have to interpret it, question it, make judgments, and make decisions. No form of measurement or analysis makes management an automatic process, but measuring a production system's performance makes managers more effective by improving the quality of their decisions.

Specifications

The starting point for controlling quality is a specification which reflects what the customer wants or needs in a product. This can begin as a subjective definition of properties — a soft ride, quick service, on-time deliveries, or accurate figures. However, subjective descriptions are of no use in building a product or providing a service. They must be translated into something specific such as physical measures.

Physical properties are usually easy to measure, but requirements like "no squeaks" or "no readily visible imperfections in the finish" must be translated into an operational definition in order to measure compliance with the specification. "Operational" means using a definite method or procedure which can be reliably repeated to make the measurement. For example, we could say a finish has "no wrinkles" if a person with 20/20 vision under specific lighting conditions cannot see any wrinkles from a distance of ten feet. Using a similar approach, even the most subjective factors such as smell can be "measured" consistently enough to be useful for controlling quality.

The need for a specification is evident where physical products are concerned, but the need is just as great in other business activities. Ideally, every product or process should have a specification so everyone knows what is required. How should a form be filled out? A package labeled? Reports organized? Parts stacked? *There are quality factors associated with every task.*

Assuming someone knows what "quality" means just because they have been doing something for years can be dangerous. People often learn by default. They may know what is wrong but not what is best. Lack of well-defined specifications will almost always result in too much or too little quality. In either case, productivity suffers. In administrative departments, this is quite common — the user of the service is not aware of the costs and the provider doesn't know exactly what's needed. In this situation, reports wind up in gold-embossed leather covers when a staple in the corner would be quite sufficient.

Preparing a specification for a product is not necessarily an easy task. Suddenly, what was taken for granted becomes a question without an obvious answer. How smooth is smooth? How closely must corners fit? What dimensional tolerance is acceptable? What response time to a service call is acceptable? Several refinements will probably be required to develop a useful specification. Even then, it must be remembered that the specification represents a point in time. Requirements may change as other parts of the process or a customer's needs change.

The best way to develop a specification is through a joint customer/vendor effort. When customers prepare specifications by themselves, they may not thoroughly understand a vendor's capabilities or the factors that affect cost and quality. Similarly, by understanding the customer's needs and uses for a product, a vendor may be able to make helpful recommendations. The customer/vendor interface is potentially very complex. Remember what was said about variety? All the relevant information about a product can't always be put on a few sheets of paper. That is why close customer/vendor relationships are so important to quality.

Since vague or non-existent specifications create waste, it is common to see quality and productivity increase several percentage points when everyone understands what is required and why. How many times have you encountered someone in your company who has said: "Gosh, I didn't know it was important to do it that way"? Any person who says that has been a source of poor quality.

It isn't always necessary to document every little thing, but it isn't difficult to note the important points of any department's operation and communicate them to those involved. Many companies do this, but it is clear many do not. *Although there may be many different ways to accomplish a task, at any given time there is only one best way.*

Summary

Statistical Process Control is not a black art and there is no reason for managers to get frightened by the word "statistics." Rather than thinking in terms of complicated statistical analysis, it is better to think in broader terms of measuring the performance of a production system, determining its capability, and identifying whether it is operating normally or not. That will determine who owns the problem — management or the operator. Controlling quality is generally an operator's responsibility but improving quality is management's job.

Measuring performance is only the first step in improving performance. Solving temporary problems or improving the process requires identifying the causes of poor quality and taking action to eliminate them. SPC is only a means to an end, not the end itself. In fact, it is certainly possible to make some improvements in the quality of a process without using any performance measures at all. It happens every day, but getting beyond obvious problems is practically impossible without quantitative information.

Some processes are complicated and there are many legitimate applications for sophisticated statistical techniques. However, most quality problems are not complex and a great deal of progress can be made with simple graphs or run charts. Beyond that, according to Kaoru Ishikawa, one of the grandfathers of SPC, 95 percent of the possible benefits can be obtained using only the basic SPC tools.[35]

Since a business is a collection of production processes, the principles of capability and control can be applied to any business activity. The methods used may vary considerably, but *measuring the performance of any process is the first step to controlling and improving it.*

CHAPTER 7

The Right Way to Solve Problems

*"Anyone can identify problems,
but few people can solve them."*

How many times have you heard somebody make this statement? Probably more than once. You may have even said it yourself. It has a certain emotional appeal, but unfortunately, it is totally wrong and probably the most costly management myth in existence. The truth is that most anyone can identify the *symptoms*, but not what is *causing* the problems.

We say someone has a problem if there is a difference between actual conditions and desired conditions. This applies to personal, business, or health problems. When we feel badly, we are reacting to the symptoms of an underlying disease such as the flu. We don't know the cause until we go to a doctor who performs some tests, compares the results with known diseases, and when a match is found, can hopefully prescribe a cure.

The same procedure should always be followed in business, but unfortunately, it isn't. A more typical pattern is to sense the symptoms of a problem, jump to a conclusion about the disease, implement a cure, and then wonder why the symptoms still persist. Either that, or it is assumed the problem is a random event and will soon go away.

The first step in solving a problem is to assume that what you sense are only symptoms and not causes. The second step is to *assume the symptoms have several root causes and that you will have to find and treat all of them if you want to solve the problem.* If you assume there is only one cause, you're probably wrong and may overlook the most important source of the problem.

The third step is to prepare a problem analysis diagram showing the logical relationship of the possible causes of the problem. Figure 7.1 is an example. Constructing a problem analysis diagram is simple. Start with the symptom and list all the factors you can think of that would contribute to it. Do your best to keep an open mind and not to jump to conclusions. Keep doing this for each successive level until you get to the point where specific corrective action could be taken. You may miss some items, but do the best you can. The quality of your diagram will depend on how well you understand the process. If you can't get past the first branch, you're in real trouble!

This diagram is similar to what is called a "cause-and-effect" or "fish-bone" diagram. I find that starting with the symptom and branching out to successive levels of detail works best for me. You can draw the diagram any way you like as long as you break the problem down into all its possible causes. For that matter, an outline format could be used. Drawing a diagram doesn't assure all possible causes will be identified, but even if it doesn't, the exercise will probably identify some possibilities that otherwise would not be considered.

The next step is to gather data to see which of the possible causes are actually creating the problem. In many cases the data will not be available and it will be necessary to run tests or set up a special system to collect the data you need. Again, the discipline of the Scientific Method should be used to link possible causes with the facts that are observed. Random

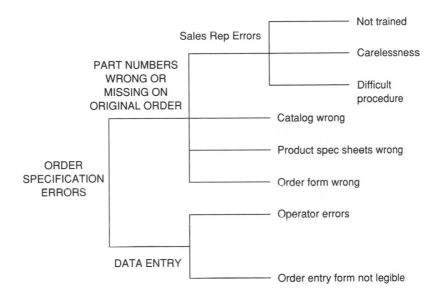

Figure 7.1 Problem Analysis Diagram

witch-hunts may occasionally be successful, but discipline and patience is the most efficient approach in the long run.

As Figure 7.1 shows, a problem that looks simple at first glance could have many causes. This diagram relates to the case discussed earlier where mismatches between controls and air conditioning units were causing production problems. By thinking through the problem of conflicting part numbers, we can determine that errors in orders could occur at many points in the process, from the catalog to the person entering the data into the computer. Assuming the problems are caused by carelessness on the part of the salesman or the person entering the order would be the typical seat-of-the-pants reaction. Those are possibilities, but not the only ones. Besides, there is initially no data to support such a conclusion.

After determining as many potential causes of incorrect part numbers as we can, the next step is to investigate previous errors. By identifying what caused a sample of previous problems, we can determine which of the potential causes is actually a culprit. By doing this, we make the following observations:

1. The catalog and specification sheets are difficult to follow. There are at least several thousand allowable combinations of features and controls. As many as twelve separate sets of numbers are needed to make a complete specification for one item.

2. The order forms do not reflect the catalog information descriptions and are incomplete. It is easy for the salesperson to omit important information because the order form does not request it. The forms have not been updated for several years.

3. When original order forms were compared with the computer data, no order entry errors were found.

4. The order entry procedure is "open-ended." That is, the system does not provide any confirmation to the salesperson or customer about what was ordered.

5. Errors are spread evenly among the salespeople. This indicates carelessness was not a problem unless all salespeople were making the same number of errors.

These findings indicate the causes of the problem are that the spec sheets are confusing, the order forms are outdated, and that specifying a product is a complicated process which is prone to error. Accordingly, the following steps can be taken to reduce the number of errors:

1. A memo can be written to everyone in the field chastising them or begging them to do better. If anyone reads it, results may improve for a week or two at most.

Not a good solution. It may be emotionally satisfying, but there is no fundamental change in the process.

2. The catalog and order forms can be redesigned to make them easier to use which would reduce the errors.

    This is an improvement in the process — a good step that would probably reduce errors considerably.

3. A copy of the entered order could be sent back to the salesman and customer to confirm it. This may catch some errors before manufacturing starts, is inexpensive, and is good practice in any case.

    Another change in the process, but not necessarily that effective because we are depending on people to check a complicated system.

4. Since the allowable combinations of air volume specifications and controls is finite, it is practical to use a computer to screen incoming orders to check for errors. It could verify that the combination of components is acceptable within the design limits of the product line. If not, it would flag the problem so corrective action could be taken before entering the order. This alternative is moderately expensive to implement and maintain, but based on the analysis of past problems, it will almost eliminate order specification errors.

    This is the best kind of solution — a permanent improvement in the process that virtually eliminates the problem.

As this example demonstrates, a simple problem can have many causes. Analyzing a problem to break it down into its possible causes prevents overlooking possibilities and making hasty assumptions. It also provides a guide for where to look, what to look for, and what data should be collected. You may not identify every potential cause on the first attempt, but by performing the analysis and then matching the facts with each of the likely causes, you will greatly improve your problem-solving efficiency.[36]

This case also illustrates how isolating the cause of a problem leads to the solution — at least for solutions 2 and 3. Solution 4 is not so obvious, but it comes from observing that correctly specifying a product is a complicated process where human errors are likely to occur. It is a complete reversal of the first solution, which says the world would be perfect if everybody wouldn't make mistakes. In practice, that philosophy doesn't work. As it becomes more difficult to perform a task correctly, quality problems will increase. *That is why improving the process improves quality and productivity, and why simply telling everyone to work harder and do a better job does not.*

People and Problems

People can be part of any problem, but the person who assumes all performance problems are created by someone who is careless or incapable will be wrong most of the time. If we look at general reasons why a task was not performed properly, it could be for any of the following reasons:

1. Poor instructions or the lack of a properly communicated specification. The person doesn't know what "right" means.
2. A specification which does not reflect the customer's needs.
3. An inherently difficult process that is prone to error.
4. Tools, equipment, or processes which are not adequate.
5. Poor quality of incoming work or raw material.
6. Insufficient training.

7. Carelessness, deliberate or otherwise.
8. The person not being capable of performing the task.

Of the possible causes, only the last two out of eight are strictly a matter of individual performance or attitude. Training is a people problem, but providing proper training is management's responsibility. The other causes are basic problems within the production system.

As the list shows, instead of assuming individual performance is causing a problem, it is best to assume the cause is some weakness in the production process itself. This not only focuses attention where it belongs, it avoids creating useless conflict between people.

So You Think You're So Good at Solving Problems?

Those who would like to test their ability to diagnose problems are invited to turn to Appendix A. This example, "Can You Analyze This Problem?" is used with permission of the *Harvard Business Review*. It is a good illustration of the confusion surrounding most problems. In fact, it is so realistic my experience indicates only about one manager in twenty reaches the right conclusion. In the real world, the success ratio would undoubtedly be higher, but one out of twenty doesn't say much for managers' ability to diagnose problems. Hence the opening paragraph of this chapter.

Developing Solutions

After identifying the fundamental causes of a problem, possible solutions must be developed. For some problems, identification of the cause leads to the solution. For others, the best solution is not so obvious.

When we talk about problems we put labels on them according to their solution. For example, if an operation is producing defective parts and increased preventive maintenance solves the problem, we say it was a "maintenance problem." On the other hand, if we change the procedure to reduce defects, we say it was a "procedural problem." Problems don't wear labels. There are only problems and possible solutions. Incorrect diagnosis of causes results in applying solutions to problems that don't exist.

Problems also don't wear nametags. The worst thing you can do when trying to solve a problem is to personalize it by blaming someone. This is sure to raise defensive hackles and make objective discussion impossible. Besides, this is jumping to conclusions. There is a difference between holding someone responsible for performance and blaming him for everything that goes wrong.

> *If you want to be successful at solving problems,*
> *make problems the common enemy,*
> *not the people who can help with the solution.*

The best solution is usually the most permanent solution. The initial cost may be higher, but in the long run, the return will be greater. One of the best ways to assure quality is to make it impossible to do something wrong. In the previous example, order entry errors could be nearly eliminated by taking advantage of logical relationships between components that make up finished products.

One of Japan's recognized authorities, Shigeo Shingo, argues that by using such techniques, the need for SPC can be eliminated and zero defects can be achieved.[37] That is certainly true in many cases, but it is also first necessary to measure performance to identify which problems need to be eliminated.

Such techniques are called *poka-yoke* by the Japanese or "mistake-proofing." Making processes mistake-proof not only eliminates problems, it frees people from having to concentrate on mundane tasks. They then have time to do something more valuable such as running another machine, learning new skills, or thinking about how to improve the process. Having to use any more effort than absolutely necessary to achieve quality is also a form of waste.

When looking for solutions, it is not enough to think about working smarter —it is just as important to think about working less.

Cross-functional Teams

Discussing solution-generating techniques such as brainstorming is beyond the scope of this book,[38] but there are two techniques that deserve attention. One is the use of cross-functional teams. This approach is especially effective because it brings many points of view to bear on a problem.

The limitations of experience on a person's vision were illustrated by a minister telling about the difficulty he had in Africa describing life in the United States. When he tried telling the natives about the houses we live in, he found it was impossible because their only word for "house" meant "mud hut." Having never seen any other structure, they could only think in terms of mud huts. When they were shown photographs of houses in the U.S., they quickly coined another word to represent this new kind of dwelling.

We're no different than these natives; we just don't want to admit it. As individuals our perspective and experience is quite limited, so while it may not boost our egos, it makes good sense to put people with different skills and experience together to find solutions to problems.

The power of this technique is shown by a story told by Dr. Russell Ackoff, a recognized authority in Operations Research. A company was having difficulty with its frozen fish. Even though it was quickly frozen at sea, the customers said it just didn't taste fresh. Keeping the fish alive in tanks on the ship seemed like the solution, but it didn't work. It seems the fish needed exercise to make them taste good (really!), and when put in the tanks, they just stayed in one place.

Mechanical devices were tried to make the fish move, but this only gave them a free ride. They didn't get any exercise and still had all the taste appeal of a mouthful of rubber bands.

An expert on fish, who just happened to be passing through the laboratory, proposed what seemed like a crazy idea. "Put a few small sharks in the tank," he suggested. "They'll eat a few fish, but they have to keep moving to breathe and the other fish will keep moving to stay out of their way." . . . . Fresh fish anyone?[39]

Forming teams that reach out vertically as well as across functions is a very effective way to develop alternative solutions to problems. Besides bringing more experience and points of view, teams also see more parts of a production process as being subject to change. To someone in manufacturing, the design of a product is fixed, but to the design engineer, it is not.

Since production begins with design, companies are increasingly getting everyone involved in the design of their products, including their vendors and customers as well as internal departments. The result is higher quality, lower costs, and shorter design cycles because many problems are recognized and solved before production begins. It doesn't take a great deal of imagination to realize that joint development of products has to produce those benefits.

None of us is as smart as all of us.

Another good reason for using cross-functional teams to solve problems is that many quality problems cut across departmental boundaries. These are probably going to be the most common and difficult problems to solve, since problems strictly within a department can be more readily attacked. Trying to find a solution to inter-departmental problems without all the players at the table will not work very well.

There are no hard and fast rules for who should be on a problem-solving team. The customer, vendor, and anyone affected by the problem should be included along with representatives of disciplines that could possibly contribute. It is also appropriate to include an outsider or two so someone will ask some "dumb questions" that may lead to solutions. Not being able to see the forest because all the trees are in the way is a real problem for everyone.

On a related subject, an acquaintance who is an executive recruiter remarked how narrow-minded most companies are when looking for managerial talent. He said he never could understand why a company would look for someone exactly like the person they just fired, but that was the usual rule. There can be some good reasons for that, of course, but should that practice be so prevalent? Had Toyota followed that line of thought, the man responsible for much of their success, Taiichi Ohno, would have never joined the company. Fortunately for them and unfortunately for Detroit, he had no experience in automobiles and no predisposition for U.S. methods.[40]

It is also important to note that when the Japanese undertook study trips to find better methods, they did not limit their trips and investigations to their own industry. They visited a wide cross section of industries, knowing they might find methods in one industry usable in another. They knew the methods found in seemingly unrelated industries could provide a competitive advantage.[41]

> *When looking for fresh ideas, the least likely place you will find them is from a person exactly like yourself.*

Cross-functional teams are very effective for both identifying the causes of problems and finding solutions to them. It is not a new concept by any means, but its value in business is being increasingly recognized. Teams can be permanent or formed on an "as needed" basis to deal with specific problems. Among other names, they have been called Quality Circles, Quality Improvement Teams, Operations Research Teams, and Task Forces. Whatever the name, they work.

However, using teams should not make managers any less accountable for their performance. There is a difference between getting help and putting your problems off on someone else. Lines of responsibility and authority should remain intact, otherwise managers may develop into buck-passers instead of problem-solvers.

Supplemental activities like Quality Circles are valuable, but their importance in Japanese companies seems to be generally exaggerated. They are not used in all companies (there are other ways of accomplishing the same ends) and where they are, they are estimated to account for no more than 10 to 30 percent of management efforts.[42] Bottom-up help is vital, but there is no substitute for good management.

Expanding the System

Another effective solution-generating technique is to expand the boundaries of the production system. Any business is made up of countless production systems, both large and small. What you call "the production system" is a matter of where you choose to draw the lines. We can think of each operation in a manufacturing plant, the entire plant, or the company as a production system. The largest "production system" includes the company, its suppliers, and its customers — with the end product being a satisfied customer. That is why having good vendors and understanding customers' needs are so important.

Just as problems inside a production system can come from outside of it, so can solutions. When the boundaries of a production system are expanded, more options for improving the process may become available. For example, one company found that it could improve the efficiency of its plants and the effectiveness of its sales force by forecasting when capacity would be available and then focusing sales efforts on the appropriate customers. Because of market conditions, this would not work every time, but it offered the possibility of correcting a range of conditions that could never be handled by the plants themselves.

Many companies have solved "quality" problems with their products by educating and assisting their customers in using them correctly. Every customer or technical service department is a tacit recognition that the customer is part of the company's production system. Production of any product or service starts when the customers place orders and ends when they are satisfied and pay the bill.

In the long run, everything in a production process can be changed, including customers, vendors, and internal operations. Cross-functional teams and expanding the boundaries of the production system are two of the most powerful ways to develop effective solutions to problems. For these techniques to work, however, management must be able to approach problems objectively and unselfishly.

For solving problems, the most valuable assets a manager can possess are two open ears and one open mind. In many cases, the problem itself may not be well-defined, let alone its solution. But even when a problem is quite clearly defined, several possible solutions may be available from inside or outside the production system.

> *When trying to identify problems and develop solutions,*
> *one word that should always be kept in mind is "maybe."*

Summary

Proper identification of all the root causes of a problem is necessary for developing effective solutions. Jumping to conclusions does more harm than good. Taking a disciplined approach by first constructing a problem analysis diagram and following that with objective analysis is the only way to be reasonably successful at identifying the fundamental causes of problems.

People can frequently be part of a performance problem, but urging people to work harder and be more careful generally avoids the real issues involved. Basic weaknesses in a production process will never be corrected by reprimands, speeches, posters, or incentives of any kind. Managers who perpetually blame everything on their employees should probably be congratulating them instead for accomplishing something worthwhile in spite of all the handicaps they must overcome.

It should be everyone's objective to find the most permanent and cost-effective way to eliminate a problem or improve a process. Thinking in terms of "Who's fault was it?" and lines on an organization chart only helps to create conflict and tunnel vision. Using cross-functional teams and expanding the boundaries of the problem are two effective ways of overcoming biases and blinders that everyone acquires over time.

CHAPTER 8

Identifying Opportunities

Perhaps the biggest mental barrier to increasing productivity and quality is not knowing what can be achieved. There isn't any easy answer to this, because most companies that get serious about improving performance exceed their goals by a wide margin. Perhaps the best answer is, "How good do you want to be?"

Even though you can't determine what can ultimately be achieved, it's helpful to identify where improvements can be made for two reasons:

1. Knowing what specific benefits are available provides an incentive to take advantage of them. After all, if you don't think you can do better, why try?
2. Having some measure of the relative value of the opportunities is necessary to establish priorities.

The following techniques are effective for finding opportunities for improving performance and estimating their potential value. Bear in mind that we are interested in the broader aspects of productivity and quality, not just cost savings and the physical product. In order to be productive, the first prerequisite is to work toward the right objectives and to do the right things.

Industry Standards

Industry standards can sometimes be used to compare one company's performance against another. This can be relevant for some large industries like steel and automobiles, but for most companies, useful figures don't exist. Company and industry performance measures can be very misleading. Unless you know precisely what the numbers mean and how they relate to your company, don't waste much time looking at industry standards.

Engineered Standards

Engineered standards are usually thought of as being a reliable definition of good performance, but they vary considerably in terms of quality. If they are not perpetually updated and verified, significant errors can quickly accumulate.

Another problem with engineered standards is the common practice of making allowances for factors such as maintenance and calibration. Allowances may be reasonable, but they are still arbitrary. In effect, they give approval to causes of waste and say nothing can be done about them. For example, a company with a well-maintained system of standards, found that during a long period of high demand it was getting 10 to 20 percent more out of its plants than predicted by the standards. This implies that for the past several years production could have been significantly higher than it had been, even though during those years the goal attainment was close to 100 percent.

Performance measures based on engineered standards also tend to drift toward 100 percent attainment because if a standard is "too high," it is easier to lower the standard than correct the problems. When this happens, performance "increases" to 100 percent and everybody feels content, even though nothing positive has been accomplished.

A more fundamental problem with engineered standards is that they only measure the basic operations of a production process and even then, only the productivity dimension. All the related operations before and after the basic tasks are ignored, omitting potentially major causes of waste, poor quality, and low productivity.

For the purposes of identifying opportunities, engineered standards can be useful, but more often than not, they reflect minimal expectations and contain significant errors. It is much better to start with no assumptions when you want to find opportunities for improving performance.

Current Tasks

The first place to look for opportunities is right at everything that's being done now. The first questions to ask are: "Why does this department exist?" and "What are its products?" For example, does Accounts Receivable exist to process paper or collect past due bills? There is a difference between activities and outputs, and it is important that the department's reason for being is clearly understood.

After the department's products and purpose are clearly understood, list all the tasks performed by the department and ask the following questions of each one:

- Is it really necessary?
- How does it support the company's strategy?
- Who is the customer receiving the goods or services?
- Has the customer specified exactly what is needed?
- Is the quantity of goods or frequency of the service too high?
- Is the quality too low or too high?
- Is there another way of accomplishing the same result?

Figure 8.1 is a worksheet for summarizing the analysis. This is a simple exercise that can yield some sizable benefits. It should be done periodically, particularly in administrative areas. As C.Northcote Parkinson observed, work really does expand to fill the time available.[43] While especially rampant

DEPARTMENT ACTIVITY ANALYSIS

TASK	CUSTOMER	WORK UNIT	UNITS/ PERIOD	REQUIRED CORE TIME	SPEC?	REDUCE QUANTITY?	REDUCE QUALITY?	ALTERNATE METHOD?
					●			
						●		
							●	
								●

Does a specification exist?
Does everyone know what is required?
Can the quantity of work be decreased?
Does it have to be done on all units all the time?
Is there too much design quality?
Can alternative methods be used to accomplish the same objective?

Figure 8.1 Department Activity Analysis Form

in the public sector, this disease is found in the business world as well. A clear definition of purpose, specific performance measures, and vigilant management is the only defense against creeping waste and inefficiency.

Work Simulation

The next step in analyzing current activities is to simulate an ideal work situation. To do this, make the work situation "ideal" in the sense that all material, machines, and so forth are precisely as they should be. Using people who are known to be competent and responsible, conduct a test for a brief time period and determine the production rate for the operation. This will establish an ideal standard for productivity (based on current practices) that can be compared to actual results to determine the "performance gap." Additional analysis can then be done to identify the components making up the gap.

This analysis is somewhat similar to a time-and-motion study approach, but it recognizes this is the level of performance a good worker could achieve under ideal conditions — not what can be expected under normal conditions. Using these figures, the minimum number of man-hours needed in a department to perform a task can be calculated. Once all the "core times" have been calculated, they can be totaled and subtracted from the time available. The difference can then be broken down into unavoidable non-productive activities and time that is either wasted or needs further analysis to be explained. Figure 8.2 is a worksheet that can be used to summarize the data for a department.

Time Usage Surveys

Time usage surveys account for how time is being spent or wasted. A form similar to Figure 8.3 can be used for this purpose. Periodically having everyone keep a detailed record of

A. Total core time required per period   127
B. Available hours per period   200
C. Non-productive hours   73

NON-PRODUCTIVE ACTIVITIES	HOURS/ PERIOD
Meetings	10
Training	12
Sick/Absent	6
TOTAL	28 (D)

D. Total identified lost hours/period   28
E. Unaccountable lost time   45   (C-D)

Figure 8.2 Department Activity Summary

their activities can be an eye-opening exercise. One such study showed foremen were spending 40 percent of their time just walking between work areas. Another discovered that highly skilled (and highly paid) machinists were using 20 percent of their time just looking for the work they were supposed to do next.

Using scarce and valuable resources for something other than their intended purpose is not confined to manufacturing

TIME USAGE SURVEY

TIME	ACTIVITY	TRAINING*	COORDI-NATING*	QUALITY*	MEETING*	OTHER
800						
815						
830						
845						
900						
915						
930						
945						
1000						
1015						
1030						
1045						

* Predefined categories that reflect what a person should be doing and known problems that can be put on the form to simplify data collection.

Figure 8.3 Time Usage Survey Form

areas. An extensive study showed an average of 25 percent of salespeople's time was spent on administrative duties.[44] No doubt, some of these subjects had complained about the administrative burden. When they did, most of them were probably told "This is part of the job." Maybe so, but such a large percentage?

Being busy is not necessarily being productive.

Time studies can provide important insight into how well people are using their time and how work is organized. *After finding out what someone is doing, the next question to ask is if that is what he or she should be doing.* Are the person's skills consistent with the task or could it be done by someone else? Is this the wisest use of the person's time and talents? Are the activities required to perform a function grouped together or spread across several departments? Time usage surveys can help identify wasted effort, fragmented tasks, and poor use of expensive resources.

A time usage survey can also shed some light on how costs should be allocated. For example, a chemical company found that its high-priced technical staff was spending 80 percent of its time on products which accounted for only 20 percent of its sales. When the true costs were known, profits on those products almost disappeared. Prices were soon changed to reflect actual costs.

Do It Yourself

A radical concept related to conducting a time survey is to actually do the job yourself! I can already hear the screams of "What, me get my hands dirty? I'm not paid to do that, someone else is." Well, maybe so, but managers are paid to find out how to make things better and if you haven't done it, the experience will probably be eye-opening.

Surprises are almost certain. Some things will be much easier than you thought and others will be much harder. For instance, one president found he could easily make three to four sales calls a day instead of the two that had become the de facto "standard" among the sales staff. In another case, an engineer who insisted all the problems with a machine were the operator's fault, quickly backed down when he tried to meet production goals himself.

However, there is much more than time estimates to be gained by getting personally involved. Information direct from the source can identify problems and opportunities that will never be seen on reports. Reports typically only reflect experience and may completely overlook new problems and opportunities. Also, any report can only convey very little information relative to the total scheme of things. The subtle relationships, the hidden meanings, the people behind the report — all of these can never be put on a sheet of paper.

As time passes, any manager's frame of reference can become obsolete. Periodically getting your hands dirty can provide a fresh perspective and valuable insight into all the problems faced by those doing the work. Managers who want to get their employees involved should recognize that involvement works both ways. Getting into the trenches occasionally is a good way to do it.

Comparative Analysis

Comparative analysis compares one machine, person, production line, or department against another. Differences in performance are obvious opportunities, but there are important limitations to this approach. First, there will always be differences in performance to some degree. This may be true for many reasons such as minor variations in product mix, equipment, or other factors that may not be evident at first glance. Also, performance could be uniformly good or bad across the units being compared and no difference would be apparent.

An additional limitation is that you must have more than one production unit to be able to make a comparison. One CEO gets around this problem by comparing notes with noncompeting European associates in his same business. Similar opportunities may be available if you look for them.

Benchmarking

Benchmarking consists of comparing yourself against the best, regardless of industry. Products, services, and performance measures might be the primary concern, but benchmarking applies to practices as well. It is very important because it is the only way to get a good view of where you stand in the world. Internal analysis cannot provide that invaluable perspective.

The nice part about benchmarking is that you know the best level of performance can actually be achieved because someone is already doing it. You also know what will make you one of the best in the business, assuming you can catch up with a moving target quickly enough. Detailed discussion of benchmarking is beyond the scope of this book. For additional information, see *Benchmarking* by Robert C. Camp listed under "References."

Historical Analysis

When comparative analysis is not practical it is always possible to compare your current performance with past performance. What is the best performance to date? What were the conditions at the time? How can these conditions be repeated? If your peak performance is 30 percent better than your average, why can't you operate closer to the peak more of the time?

Comparative and historical analysis can provide very useful information for identifying opportunities. However, it is first necessary to have the data available for making comparisons. Unfortunately, useful data may not exist when you start. The value of having a good historical performance database is usually not recognized until it is needed.

Flowcharting

Preparing a detailed flowchart of current operations provides no quantitative information about opportunities, but it is a very valuable exercise. This can reveal processes and procedures that don't make sense anymore — or maybe never did. Bottlenecks, duplicate efforts, and unnecessarily complicated procedures are the types of opportunities frequently uncovered by flowcharting. Taking the pieces apart and putting them back together can yield some very worthwhile improvements.

The value of flowcharting should not be underestimated, but for it to be useful, it must be done correctly and thoroughly to a fine level of detail. Every step, operation, and decision must be carefully identified and noted. It may take several days to document what appears to be a simple process.

Flowcharting may be more effective when performed by someone who isn't familiar with the production process because that person is more likely to ask "dumb" questions.

Figure 8.4 is an example of a flowchart. The form and the symbols used aren't critical, although it is good practice to use conventional symbols. What matters is that all the activities, exceptions, loops, and decision points are first identified and then questioned. Just because "it has always been done that way" doesn't mean that's the best way to do it. The value isn't so much in the final chart, but in the questions and thoughts that arise as it is being developed.

Complaint Files

Another useful source of information is customer complaint files. These usually seriously understate the extent of a

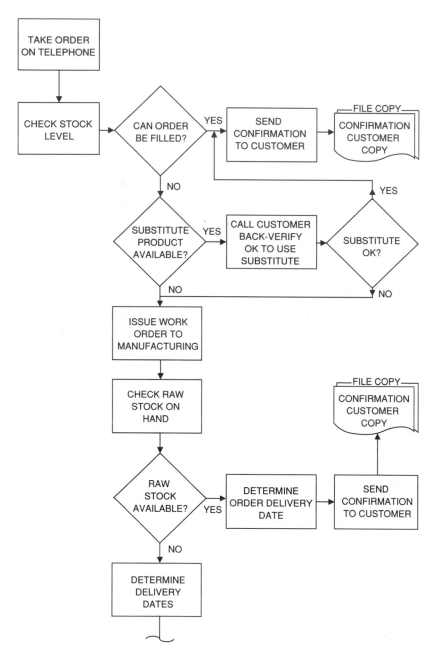

Figure 8.4 Flowchart Sample

quality problem, but they can indicate chronic weaknesses in the production system and what the customer wants. When reviewing complaint files, remember that the information may be symptomatic and not very accurate. Still, it is well worth the effort.

Waste Analysis

Waste is any resource not converted to a useful product or output. Mention waste and images of scrap and defective parts come to mind. But that is only the tip of the iceberg. If all business waste was as visible and smelly as garbage, you can be sure managers would be working harder to eliminate it.

Business waste comes in many forms:

- Defective products and scrap
- Rework (anything not done right the first time)
- Inventory, including work-in-process (having more than you need)
- Time (downtime, setup time, delay time)
- Motion (more motion than necessary to accomplish a task)
- Movement (moving materials more than necessary)

These are more or less tangible forms of waste, but there are other kinds which are harder to see:

- People without the tools and information to do their jobs correctly
- People without the skills to use the tools they have
- People with skills that aren't being used
- People with brains who aren't allowed to use them
- Managers spending too much time on trivial matters
- Managers making decisions others could make
- More quality in anything than is necessary to get the job done

- Meetings that don't communicate, decide, or solve problems
- Reports that aren't used because they don't contain useful information

This is by no means a complete list. Unfortunately, recognizing waste is as much an art as it is a science. The other procedures given here can help identify waste, but it is also a matter of getting people to recognize waste for what it is. That is management's job through training, setting an example, and clearly communicating what matters and what doesn't.

Operations Variance Analysis

An easy and effective method to identify many problems in a process is to conduct an operations variance analysis (hereafter called a "variance analysis"). Here, the focus is not on how to do a task better, but on the faults in the process which prevent a task from being done as intended. This approach is particularly effective at finding problems occurring between steps in a production process. A variance analysis will not tell you what level of performance can ultimately be reached. Its strength is that it will point out many costly problems that are not being recognized or are being ignored.

A variance is anything that deviates from normal or desired conditions. In other words, it is anything that isn't the way it ought to be. It is non-conformance to ideal conditions as seen by the person doing the task. Some examples of variances are: (1) mislabeled materials; (2) incorrect instructions in a test procedure; and (3) customer inquiries not answered correctly, which create a problem for the salesperson on the next call.

Variances are quality problems. As such, a *variance always results in a real cost,* even though it may not be recognized at the time. Any deviation from the ideal point must cost something, no matter how small. Variances can come from any place in a production process, but they are most evident where work is passed from one person to another.

An interesting point about variances is that they also cause some form of emotional stress in the people who have to deal with them. In effect, a physical problem creates a psychological problem. Frustration and aggravation are good indicators of variances. An easy way to identify them is to listen to everyone complain about the things that make their jobs more difficult. How many times have you heard someone make comments like:

- "These salespeople can't ever fill out the orders right!"
- "Why can't the store managers send the payroll records in on time?"
- "How can we build the parts when the drawing isn't complete?"

Such complaints are indicators of real problems that shouldn't be ignored. They increase costs, cause emotional stress, and can lead to serious personal conflict when someone relieves their stress by unloading on the nearest warm body.

During a study of how automobile production line workers coped with their jobs, one of the loudest complaints was about parts that wouldn't fit.[45] The people on the line couldn't do their jobs properly because someone else hadn't done theirs. What's also interesting about this article is that it was written in 1974 and has turned out to be an unwitting prediction of the decline of the domestic auto industry. Why didn't management correct the problems? Probably because they were making plenty of money at the time and the problems seemed unimportant.

No one likes to work at a job that is a constant aggravation. Consequently, the best people to report variances are the ones receiving them because they have a selfish interest in making their jobs easier. Figure 8.5 illustrates the reporting system. *By using this technique, each department or person becomes a point of inspection for the preceding department(s), providing a system of checks and balances throughout the production system.* In effect, everyone becomes an inspector without any additional cost. But remember, the point is not to inspect quality into the product, but to identify problems and weaknesses in the process so they can be corrected.

Variances are one of the most important factors to measure in any production process for the following reasons:

1. They are a source of waste and cost. Every variance costs something in terms of quality or the effort to correct it.
2. Variances are quality problems. Identifying variances forces the development of a quality standard or specification for each operation. The first step is to say something is wrong; the next step is to define what's right.
3. They create personal stress and conflict between departments. There is a real cost attached to these problems in terms of tardiness, absenteeism, employee turnover, and the time spent by managers in keeping the peace.

Variances can come from inside a work group as well as from outside, but internal variances get addressed more quickly than those passed from one group to another. Internal variances are controllable within the group. Those coming from external sources are seen as beyond control of the group — and they usually are. As mentioned earlier, this is one reason cross-functional teams can be so effective.

Passing problems to someone else is a game played by many people in any company. It is management's job to make sure this does not happen. Frequently, the single

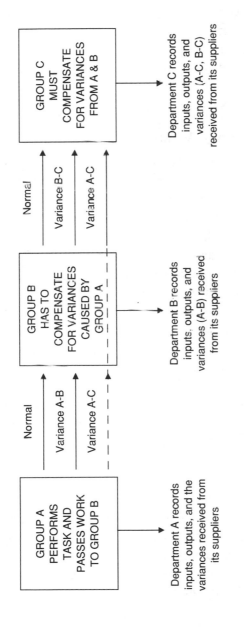

Each group records its work inputs, work outputs, and the quality of materials and services it receives from supporting groups. Quality measures include formally defined product requirements and operational variances that interfere with performing a task as it should be performed.

Figure 8.5 Variances in a Production Process and How They Can Be Measured

biggest reason a department is not operating efficiently is that it is spending much of its time compensating for problems passed to it from other departments. Saying, "Don't tell me your problems, your job is to overcome them," is a way of avoiding the issue. The correct approach is to measure the problems being passed around and hold the departments creating them accountable for reducing them.

Conducting a Variance Analysis

Performing a variance analysis is simple in concept, but it may be difficult in practice if there is any friction between managers, workers, or work groups. For this reason, using someone outside the affected departments to conduct the analysis can sometimes be helpful.

The first step is to prepare a form similar to Figure 8.6. The next step is to explain to everyone concerned that the purpose of the exercise is to identify problems so they can be reduced and not to point fingers at anyone. Then ask *everyone* to write down *everything* that (1) isn't the way they think it should be or (2) creates a problem for them in doing their job. Emphasis should be placed on any factor that has already been identified as critical for the company. For example, if order cycle time is important, then anything causing delays or other time-consuming problems would be considered a variance. The best rule to follow is, "If in doubt, write it down."

Two or three attempts may be necessary to get good data because most everyone tends to be insensitive to problems during the initial studies. They have seen the problems for so long, they seem like old friends. After collecting this information for a few days, recurring problems will be quite apparent. By counting the number of occurrences in each category and estimating the cost of one occurrence, the total cost of each variance can be determined.

NAME _Hugo Mumsquart_ DEPT _Final Assy_ DATE _7·7·90_

VARIANCE	SOURCE (DEPT)	IMPACT	NOTES
Page 2 of J48 drawing missing	Eng.	Wait 15 min. for new one	
1/4-20 screws missing — J48	Inventory	10 min.	
Burrs on side panel J48	?	20 min. to remove/retouch	Happens all the time
Issued wrong hinges for J492	Inventory	15 min. lost	
Burrs on H366 cover	?	Set job aside	see?
H400 corner brace bent	?	scrapped & replaced	think forklift ran over it

Figure 8.6 Variance Survey Form

Purchasing Materials and Services

A limiting factor to any production process is the quality of the incoming work and raw material. *No matter how good internal performance may be, poor quality inputs will limit the quality of the output and the efficiency of a production process.*

Since it is common for manufacturers to spend 50 percent or more of their sales dollar on purchased items, it could be assumed that a corresponding amount of quality problems come from vendors. Even service companies are not immune to problems from vendors since they also use purchased materials and services.

Poor quality in any material or service used to produce a product must result in rework or some other cost. Not recognizing this and buying on price alone leads to suboptimization and higher total costs. The cheapest product does not necessarily result in the lowest total cost to a company.

The first step in looking for opportunities in purchased goods or services is to determine what you need and prepare a specification. If you don't understand your requirements or if you haven't communicated them to your vendors, how do you expect them to provide you with what you need? The same principle applies to internal vendors as well.

A variance analysis will probably bring some problems with purchased materials to light, but not all of them. Just identifying problems with purchased parts can be a time-consuming task, let alone solving them. Data on delivery performance should be available from purchasing and accounts payable records. Quality data, however, may be totally lacking except for glaring problems which resulted in returns. In that case, it will be necessary to start collecting relevant data to develop some useful information. Ultimately, a specification will have to be developed and an audit performed on each product and vendor to determine problems and priorities.

Don't forget that what applies to your vendors also applies to you when you wear your vendor hat. Do you know what your customers think of your quality? How do you compare to your competition? The best way to find out is to ask. You may not like what you hear, but it is better to know you have a problem and deal with it than to let it solve itself by losing the customer. (More will be said about vendor/customer relationships in Chapter 11 on managing performance.)

Summary

Healthy profits do not mean performance cannot be improved. The business cemetery is full of tombstones with the epitaph:

We were making so much money, what went wrong?

Successful companies and successful managers continuously look for ways to get better. These methods for finding opportunities can be used in nearly any business activity to find opportunities for improving performance and to estimate their potential value. Every one of the applicable methods should be used, because each one looks at the production process from a different perspective.

However, there are two important things to keep in mind about the results. First, the figures obtained from the analysis only reflect current practices. Second, they only provide a starting point. By no means do the findings represent either all the opportunities available or maximum limits of performance, especially since improvement should never stop. As many companies have demonstrated, when they got serious about improving performance, more was achieved than anyone thought was possible.

CHAPTER 9

The Importance of Culture

U p to this point, we have been primarily concerned with the technical aspects of improving performance. However, since everything happens through people, the human side of the equation is at least as important as the technical side. Probably more so. As the quality director of one company said, "When I started, I thought this job would be 75 percent numbers and 25 percent people. After two years, I know it's the other way around."

How people act and interact depends on what and how they think. This is a product of their beliefs, values, and knowledge which is called a "culture." Companies have different cultures just as surely as countries and tribes do. Aggressive, passive, dictatorships, benevolent kingdoms, democracies — you can find companies with management styles and values of all descriptions.

A company's culture limits the level of performance it can achieve. It is well known that the work environment affects individual performance, but that is only the tip of the iceberg. The wrong culture also greatly reduces the quality of decisions, how well technical tools will be used, and the rate of progress a company can make.

For example, a manager who believes his job is to give orders and reprimand people is not likely to listen to problems, complaints, and ideas from those who report to him. As Tom Gelb, vice president of continuous improvement for Harley-Davidson experienced, attempting a participative program like Quality Circles in an autocratic environment doesn't work very well.[46] Similarly, a manager who has been punished for trying and failing in the past is not going to try anything new again. Although it is not often recognized, *there is a very strong cause-and-effect relationship between a company's culture, what it can do, and how it gets things done.*

The Quality Culture

Since culture affects performance, is there such a thing as the ideal culture? There may be, but exactly what it is hasn't been determined yet. However, there are cultural characteristics that are generally recognized as being critical.

First and foremost is the desire to always get better, to never be satisfied with less than perfection, and to be the best. Improving quality and productivity is a continuous process, but that only happens if someone drives it. Continuous improvement starts with a state of mind. It is the difference between "If it ain't broke, don't fix it" and "It's working well — how can we make it better?" Nobody ever improved their capabilities without first wanting to.

To improve performance, however, a company must be willing to change, to learn, and be receptive to new ideas. It must also be willing to take reasonable risks and invest in research and learning with no guarantee of success or a return. All of these factors depend upon management, not the workers.

A long-term outlook is a vital component because it affects how a company relates to its customers, vendors, and employees. A company that sees its relationship with its customers as never-ending, behaves quite differently than one which is concerned only about tomorrow's sale. Similarly, a long term company sees its suppliers as an extension of itself and a cooperative partner instead of an adversary to keep off-balance.

Employees in the long term company are seen as an asset instead of a variable cost. This, in turn, makes a big difference in personnel management and policies. It places a higher premium on not over-staffing, selecting the best employees, continually upgrading skills, and keeping everyone employed. No company likes to lose a capable employee, but with a short term outlook, there is little incentive to develop the skills and knowledge of employees.

Quality improvement almost always initially requires taking some short term losses in favor of long term gains. If management always wants to see results tomorrow from what is done today, that will be reflected in everyone's actions. For true long term success, management must get everyone to focus on doing the right things, not just on costs and profits. In other words, put more emphasis on the process and less on short term results. It is true that results pay the bills, but management must accept that doing the right things in the short run will pay off in the long run. This is one of the central points in the "Kaizen" or continuous improvement philosophy.[47]

Taking a long term view is especially important when looking for solutions to problems. It is almost always possible to make a temporary patch that will provide some quick relief to a problem. Pressure to produce short term results will encourage this behavior in two ways. First, it encourages reacting to symptoms instead of taking the time to identify the causes. Second, even if the causes are identified, the quick patch will be favored over permanently improving the process. Short term thinking gets in the way of finding the best solutions to problems.

Finally, taking a long term perspective encourages taking a broader view of the business. If a company or a department is working toward the wrong objectives, it is not productive no matter how efficient it may be. Identifying the right objectives is not all that easy in the best of circumstances, but if management is looking only six months ahead, it is practically impossible.

Another important cultural ingredient is *mutual respect, trust, and credibility throughout the company*. Without credibility and trust, effective communication up, down, and across the organization is impossible. Instead of receiving information that is complete and reliable, managers will receive information that has been filtered and distorted. Furthermore, when they communicate, what their audience hears may be quite different from what is being said.

Trust comes from being honest and candid. It also comes from admitting your mistakes and letting others fail without handing them their heads. When employees are afraid of their superiors, their superiors will only hear carefully selected and shaped information. This applies to CEOs as well as line supervisors. Managers who adopt an autocratic or belligerent style need to recognize that their actions will only make their job more difficult.

> *It's tough to make good decisions in the real world*
> *when your information is coming from Disneyworld.*

Credibility results from doing what you say you will do — or at least giving a good explanation for why you didn't. Unfortunately, credibility and trust are in short supply in many companies. According to a 1987 report in *The Wall Street Journal*, 78 percent of American workers are suspicious of management to some degree.[48] Similarly, a 1989 survey of 400 managers showed that one-third of them distrust their own direct bosses and 55 percent don't believe top management.[49] Those are not encouraging figures, but they can be changed.

It is not enough for managers to be trusted by their employees; managers must also trust and respect their employees. If managers don't trust their employees, they will not hear important information because they won't be listening. Trust and credibility is a two-way street.

A story that demonstrates the value of trust and credibility occurred in a manufacturing plant where the machine operators were asked to report "wipeouts." A wipeout was defined as a large amount of waste or rejects. These problems happened very infrequently, so when they did, it was important to get as much information as possible about the incident.

In one such case, the operator had simply forgotten to set up the machine properly, sending $500 down the drain in 15 minutes. She promptly wrote it down on the log, noting that the cause of the error was: "I screwed up. Forgot to...because I didn't use the checklist."

As he was passing through the plant, a visitor from Germany happened to see the entry and asked what it was all about. When it was explained, he was flabbergasted! "You mean," he said, "this girl threw away $500 and she had the nerve to report on herself? What is going to happen to her?" When it was explained that the only thing that would happen was that she would be thanked for being so honest, the poor fellow almost had a heart attack! His reply was, "That would never happen in our company!" How unfortunate. That's what trust and credibility are all about. It's also about the fact that a lot of time was not wasted trying to track down a fictitious machine problem.

Personal identification with the company is necessary for there to be more than passive acceptance of goals, plans, and activities. "Identification" means more than saying, "I work for Fubart Corporation." It means individuals see a link between their interests and the company's interests. It is the result of the company being able to provide a good answer to the question, "What's in it for me?"

If employees do not see themselves as an important part of a company, their participation in activities like suggestions and problem-solving teams will be minimal. In addition, it is important for people to relate to a higher objective than their own immediate interest when solving problems. Without a good amount of unselfishness, approaching problems objectively and finding the best solution for the company is difficult for anyone.

One of the key elements in developing personal identification with the company is an understanding of how a business works. "Profit" is still a dirty word to the average worker and most of them have serious misconceptions of what business is all about.[50] The only way to clear up these misunderstandings is through education in basic business principles and the company's operations. It seems that as a minimum, all employees need to be aware of the basic economic facts of life: without profits there are no raises, no benefits, and ultimately no jobs.

Some companies go so far as to teach all of their employees how to read an income statement and balance sheet. Then they regularly keep everyone updated on the company's position. Jack Stack, CEO of Springfield Remanufacturing Center Corporation does this and calls it "The Great Game of Business." He contends it is an important mechanism to get people to come into work every morning and enjoy it! Judging from his results, it's difficult to argue with him.[51]

Employees also need to know where they fit in the scheme of things and how their efforts contribute to their company's success. How not to do it was illustrated by a company which made small mechanical controls. On his way to his exit interview after thirty years of work, a retiring employee happened to stop at a salesman's cutaway display of a control. Noting his interest, the personnel manager asked him what he found so interesting. The employee said, "You know, I've been making those disks for thirty years. I must have made millions of them and this is the first time I ever knew what they were used for."

That story is all too typical of both white-collar and blue-collar employees the world over. How can people feel like they are part of a team when they don't understand the game and what they contribute? It may be more difficult to create a feeling of belonging in a large company than a small one, but large companies certainly don't have a monopoly on doing a poor job of it. It's not just good for morale. When employees understand how they contribute, their ability to contribute increases.

However, knowing the game and the part one plays isn't enough to make a person feel like he or she is a true participating member of a company. *There has to be an economic link to the company's success as well.* Pirates used to get a share of the plunder, and even a pack of wolves shares the kill. Why shouldn't an employee expect to share in the fortunes of the company? As John Mariotti, President of Huffy Bicycles said: "People are willing to get involved but after a while they start looking to see 'where's the beef?'"[52]

Some companies share their success with annual profit sharing plans. Others use short term incentive plans, and others, like Nucor, use a combination of plans for hourly employees and management. One company takes the novel approach of determining what percentage of profits it needs to retain and distributes the rest to its employees. Perhaps the simplest scheme is to set aside a fixed percentage of profit that is shared on a pro-rata basis based on each person's annual earnings.

Companies that want their employees to be loyal and do their best must share their success with the people who produce that success. While the best method is not evident, there are certainly many workable options. How well American companies share their success is debatable, but one Japanese visitor remarked: "I get the impression that American managers spend more time worrying about the well-being and loyalty of their stockholders, whom they don't know, than about their workers, whom they do know...Japanese managers are always asking themselves how they can share the company's success with their workers."[53]

Getting employees to identify themselves with their company takes good communication, awareness of how a business and the company works, understanding the contribution a person makes, and participation in the company's fortunes. By no means are the Japanese the only ones who have been able to do this, but they have been particularly successful at it. As one observer commented, "In Japan, people don't work for the company; they *are* the company."[54] That feeling not only generates enthusiasm and energy, it also leads to cooperation, good communication, and unselfishness.

Employee involvement is an important part of the quality culture because it improves:

- The quality of decisions
- The effectiveness of solutions to problems
- The validity of plans and how quickly they can be implemented
- The morale and productivity of the entire organization

"Employee involvement" might be defined several ways, but its central theme is to make the people affected by a decision responsible for the decision. This is accomplished by letting everyone affected participate in making the decision. Ideally, that means letting them make the decision. Employee involvement has many forms. Quality Circles, Quality Improvement Teams, teamwork, suggestion systems, and participative management are all ways of getting employees (including managers) involved in improving performance.

Employee involvement improves the quality of decisions by improving the quality and quantity of information available to decision makers throughout the company. Since the person doing the work knows more about his or her problems than anyone else, every employee is a source of valuable and unique information. This information is rarely available from a company's formal communication channels.

General Electric found out what first-hand information was worth when it introduced a new refrigerator compressor motor. Some of the people doing the qualification tests were questioning the results, but because of pressure to get into production, no one wanted to be the bearer of bad news. Upper-level management, only seeing well-filtered reports, was completely unaware of the problems suspected by the test technicians. Over a million units were shipped before the problems began surfacing in the field. As a result, GE took a pre-tax write-off against earnings of $450 million in 1988. In retrospect, the division's head of manufacturing and technology said he would have "...found the lowest damn level people we had..and just sat down in their little cubbyholes and asked them 'How are things today?'"[55]

That was an expensive conversation that didn't happen. No doubt there have been many others. It illustrates why "Management By Walking Around" can be so valuable. There are, however, other ways to accomplish the same results. A simple method is to have those involved in a critical decision sign off on it, taking that down to the lowest practical level. That is standard procedure in many situations. In the GE case, it would mean that the technicians who conducted the tests would have been asked to certify that they had no reservations about the results or the readiness of the product for production. Of course, if management applies subtle pressures to inhibit free expression, such efforts are worthless.

Employee involvement not only helps avoid problems, it also produces better solutions by bringing more brainpower to bear on them, just as cross-functional teams do. Even within a single department there is a wide range of experience and perspectives. The "dumb" question, "wild" idea, "silly" suggestion, or offhand comment may not be the solution, but it can trigger thoughts and discussion which leads to one. Not using this potentially rich source of ideas is a real waste of human talent.

The quality of planning is also improved by employee involvement. Just as the people doing the work know more about their problems, so will they know the most about how plans will impact them. Giving everyone affected the chance to be heard while plans are being developed can avoid costly problems or eliminate them before they occur. It also paves the way for smooth implementation. Thoroughly reviewing plans in advance lets everyone know what is expected of them. It also gives everyone a chance to buy into the decision so it will not be opposed during implementation.

One way or another, the time to review plans and coordinate activities is going to be spent. Isn't it more sensible to spend it up front and avoid problems instead of plunging ahead and solving them later? As in everything else, it is always more productive to do it right the first time. The Japanese are well-known for their supposedly "slow" decision making but rapid implementation.

Another reason why involvement is important is that people want to be in on things and feel their thoughts and ideas are valuable. These are important motivating factors.[56] When, by being ignored, you are told that you and your thoughts don't count, it is hard to feel like a valued member of any group.

Employee involvement is not simply a suggestion system or monthly speeches. Nor is it a motivational trick or game managers can play. It is everything that results from a sincere belief that every employee is valuable and has something worthwhile to contribute. Such actions as giving up reserved parking places and eating in the same lunchroom can be meaningful, but without a change in managers' attitudes, they are only empty gestures. One employee said it all when his company was being introduced to the "teamwork" concept:

> "I'd like to have input into my job, but when that work-group manager said 'I've got 51 percent of the decision-making [power],' that was the end of that."[57]

Employee involvement is not democratic management. It doesn't mean everyone votes on all decisions. It does mean employees of all ranks are kept informed, given the chance to be heard on decisions that affect them, and are given as much freedom and responsibility as possible. Employee involvement is also not "warm and fuzzy" management or "anything goes" management. To the contrary, a high level of autonomy cannot be granted without making it clear that a corresponding high level of performance is required.

The quality culture also needs *decentralized management and decision making*. That means putting decisions as close to the action as possible, not as close to the top as possible. Like employee involvement, decentralization improves quality through better information, better decisions, quicker response, better solutions, ownership of decisions, and improved morale. With decentralized management, more gets done because more decisions are made. At any level, managers who don't delegate become bottlenecks and roadblocks to progress. Not only that, they are working too hard.

A case in point was a small chemical company where little progress was being made in installing new production control systems. The answer to every question was: "Henry (the CEO) will have to answer, check, or approve that." When

Henry was asked why his managers could not make those decisions, his reply was: "Those guys can't make decisions. They don't know how to. I've always had to make all the decisions. I don't know why I have to decide everything around here when I have all these people on the payroll." The answer to his question, of course, is that by never letting his managers make decisions, they never learned how. Instead, after teaching his managers for several years that they weren't capable, they believed it.

Lack of authority and freedom to do even the simplest things is a sensitive issue at middle management levels. Top management often sees middle managers as mere implementers, holding them accountable for results but giving them no authority. Anything they want to do requires several layers of approval, typically from people who don't understand their problems. Not surprisingly, they feel helpless, worthless, and bitter about their situation.

I find it amazing (and discouraging) how many division managers, plant managers, and general managers of remote manufacturing facilities feel that way. "They don't trust me to spend $50" and "I can only do what I'm told" are typical comments. The truly sad part about these situations is that these spiritless people are supposed to be leading and motivating hundreds of other employees. Surely, there is a way to grant managers in these situations some level of autonomy so they don't feel they are being treated like mindless robots.

Effective delegation, or empowerment, is accomplished by clearly defining boundaries of accountability and authority as well as what is expected. Holding people responsible for performance measures over which they have no control will not work. Neither will giving them the authority, but not the information and tools they need to do the job. Recognition and reward must also be consistent with responsibilities and performance. Whether someone is in charge of a division, a department, or a work team, the empowerment package must be clear, consistent, and complete.

As mentioned earlier, one of the biggest barriers to effective delegation is the fear of losing control. This can be relieved by having good performance measures in place. Another obstacle to delegation is the fear of losing power and status. Managers who are used to giving orders, keeping secrets, and behaving as policemen are going to be threatened when they are asked to become teachers, coordinators, and facilitators. Managers who see delegation and employee involvement as a threat to their power must realize they are only exchanging the power of position for the power of knowledge and persuasion. That is easier said than done. When you've had your hand on the throttle for years, it is hard to let go.

Piecework Pay Systems

Piecework pay systems can only be used where the work is quite repetitive and homogeneous, but they are fairly widespread. They deserve special attention because piecework systems limit performance and illustrate the relationship between culture, management methods, and behavior.

Piecework pay systems typically use standards developed by industrial engineers as the basis for paying workers for each unit produced. This seems like a reasonable approach, but in practice there are problems with both the standards and the method of managing performance:

1. *Workers do not usually consider the standards accurate and objective, creating conflicts between management and workers.* These conflicts can have serious effects. One company always had good relations with its employees until a pay system based on engineered standards was installed. Productivity increased initially, but after a few years, conflicts and distrust developed. Productivity actually went down, while wages went

up. The bad feelings ultimately led to a union coming into the company.

2. *Peer pressure against "rate busters" actually limits output.* In addition, since high rates will be contested and low ones will not, there is a bias toward lower productivity standards. There is some incentive to work harder, but there is also an incentive to learn how to manipulate the system.

3. *Quality will suffer in favor of productivity.* Piecework sends the clear message that only quantity counts. Making someone rework their mistakes sounds like a good solution, but remember, only the defects actually found will be corrected.

4. *The system emphasizes working harder, instead of improving the production process.* Not only that, if anyone finds a better way to do something so they can increase their income, they have a vested interest in keeping it to themselves. If they share it with everyone else, the base rate will increase and they will lose their advantage.[58]

5. *The system lowers a person's self-image.* In effect, a piecework system tells employees that they are the equivalent of a machine; they are valued only because they can produce so many units an hour. Deming feels strongly about the issue, saying that systems of standards rob the individual of his dignity and desire to produce good work.[59] Piecework pay systems also rob managers of their motivation to manage. The subconscious thought is "If we pay according to the standard, the people will manage themselves." Not true.

6. *A person being paid solely on individual effort is not likely to feel like a member of a team.* When talking with people on piecework pay systems, their sense of individ-

uality becomes quite apparent. How do you make people think of the common good when they perceive themselves as hired guns?

7. *The pressure of having to meet the day's quota to earn a decent wage creates emotional stress.* This is especially true when problems outside the person's control interfere with their work. They feel they are being cheated by being made to pay for others' mistakes and rightly so. This causes destructive conflicts between individuals and departments.

8. *Piecework pay systems limit the flexible use of a company's most important resource, its people.* They put handcuffs on employees, but they also put chains on management. Allen-Edmonds, a shoe manufacturer, eliminated its piecework system and saw productivity increase 20 percent! Much of this increase was attributed to being able to use people when and where they could be used best.[60]

9. *Piecework pay systems discourage change.* A change made to a process can disrupt a stable situation and cause a temporary loss of wages. Setting the new standard can then result in management feeling it is giving too much and workers feeling that they are being cheated. Since change is threatening for everyone, an incentive is created to keep things the same. These feelings may be subconscious, but they are still present in everyone's mind.

There aren't many good things to say about piecework pay systems. The people administering these systems would probably never stand for being treated the same way, but old ideas don't die easily. As Wickham Skinner says:

Pressure for output and efficiency are the staples of factory life as hourly workers experience it. Engineers and supervisors tell them what to do, how to do it, and how long they may take. Theirs is an often unhappy, quota-measured culture — and has been for more than 150 years. In such an environment, even the most reasonable requests are resented.[61]

Piecework systems stem from the belief that people are the source of all quality and productivity problems, that money is the sole motivator, and that people can't be trusted to do their best. Few companies using a piecework system would take that viewpoint to extremes, but those beliefs are somewhere in the minds of managers, sometimes so embedded that management can't even conceive of any other way to operate.

As an alternative, consider an environment where it is assumed everyone does their best, where everything is reported honestly and objectively, and the minimum performance standards are essentially what has been achieved in the past. Then, instead of spending management and staff time managing standards, negotiating conflicts, and blaming people, these energies can be used for improving the production system. In such an environment, changes to methods and procedures are readily accepted because no one has anything to lose and everyone has something to gain if performance improves. This kind of environment cannot exist with piecework pay systems.

Still, many companies have seen productivity increase by using such pay systems. Where no management system existed before, which is often the case, that would not be surprising. But in the long run, piecework systems discourage precisely what they are designed to encourage — higher worker productivity.[62]

Changing Culture

Fortunately, cultural traits are learned and not genetically inherited. Unfortunately, it can take a long time to change the way people think — especially when their beliefs are ingrained. One of the most difficult situations is where workers and management have been fighting for years. Even in those cases, minds can be changed.

At Cyprus Mines in Arizona, it took only a year to make a significant change in the company's culture. Where there was once continual management/union conflict, there is now manager/employee cooperation (and no union). The key element in this dramatic turnaround was that management changed its approach first. Managers were sent to "charm school," work rules were changed, raises given, and the workplace made safer. Workers' initial doubts and fears quickly evaporated when management took the lead.[63]

Cyprus Mines may hold a record for making so much change in so little time, but even it still has more road to travel. The time it takes to overhaul a company's culture is better measured by years than months. It took A.O Smith eight years to progress from Quality Circles to getting the unions involved in making decisions.[64] Harley-Davidson's cultural evolution started in 1978. Considerable progress was made over the years, but it wasn't until the late 1980s that management realized it had to make a major change in how it related to employees and the union structure.[65]

What the CEO and top executives of a company say, and more importantly do, affects the entire organization. Employees respond to their total environment, not just to the few selected speeches, meetings and memos that top management chooses to share during a year. Actions do speak louder than words. Twisting the truth and talking out of both sides of the mouth doesn't work. Too many companies tell their employees:

- We care (when it's convenient and doesn't cost anything).
- We share (if there is anything left after we get ours).

- We're a team (but guess who gets hurt the most when times get tough).
- We want your opinions and ideas (as long as they agree with ours).
- Think (but always do it by the book).
- Be responsible (but never do anything without checking with me first).
- Try something new (but it better work or you'll regret it).

A particularly sore point in U.S. companies is compensation for CEOs. According to *Industry Week*, the CEO of a large U.S. company makes an average of 35 times as much as an average manufacturing employee, compared to 15 times in Japan and 20 in Europe.[66] In particular, U.S. auto executives are paid much more than their Japanese counterparts. In view of continued trade deficits and decreases in U.S. market share, the high U.S. salaries certainly don't appear to be justified. According to some experts in the field, such big pay gaps stimulate employees to produce "all the kinds of negative and dangerous behavior they [the companies] don't want and none of the behavior they do want."[67]

American workers are told to perform if they want to get paid but they see different rules applied at the top. They also see such wonderful examples of rewarding performance as a company laying off thousands of workers one week and the top executives giving themselves 30 percent pay raises the next. There are also many examples of CEOs walking off with fat severance awards after running their companies into the ground.

Few people would say individuals like David Packard of Hewlett-Packard or Ken Iverson of Nucor don't deserve the financial rewards they have received: they have created well-paying jobs for people, dividends for shareholders, and taxes for governments. In many other cases, it appears corporate America has lost sight of what capitalism is all about. Hopefully, the countries being freed of the yoke of Communism will pick the right examples to follow.

If conflicting signals are sent from above, they will be apparent to everyone below. Managers at all levels need to recognize that the lowest paid and newest employee is smart enough to know when he or she is being told a fairy tale. The common sense of common people should not be underestimated by managers who ought to be smart enough to know better. As the Sheriff said in "The Best Little Whorehouse in Texas:"

> "I may not be very sophisticated, but I'm smart enough to know when someone is peeing on my boots and calling it a rainstorm!"

The point is that a company's culture cannot be changed by speeches, posters, and gimmicks. "Do as I say, not as I do" will not work. Culture is beliefs and values. When top management changes the way it sees customers, vendors, and employees, thoughts and actions throughout the company will change accordingly. Once attitudes change at the top, it will not take long for that change to filter down through the entire organization.

There are no sure-fire or painless ways to change a company's culture. Very clearly, the first step is for management to recognize the need and have the desire to change. Beyond that, professional help is readily available in disciplines such as team building, employee involvement, resolving conflicts, and group problem-solving. Outside assistance can be very helpful, especially where there are deep-seated fears and attitudes. However, changing culture will always be primarily an inside job.

Japanese Versus American Culture

A discussion of culture would not be complete without addressing the issue of national cultures, because broader environmental factors have some effect on how managers think. Certainly not all Japanese or American managers think alike, but there are some valid generalizations which illustrate the link between culture and behavior.

In the U.S., the corporate raider, the overnight success, the dramatic turnaround, and the superstar manager (who may turn out to be tomorrow's flaming meteor) have been the subject of countless articles in the best business publications. Who has not read a story about the turnaround artist, entrepreneur, or manager who's motto is: "Ready, fire, aim"? This cliche has become so time-worn, any writer who uses it should be forced to stand in front of a real firing squad!

That such stories are appealing is no surprise given our national heritage of rebellion, rugged individualism, and doing things on a grand scale. Unfortunately, stories like this influence the way American managers think. As Rosabeth Kanter, editor of *Harvard Business Review* said: "American business has become obsessed with heroes, enamored of bold moves, and addicted to high drama. Mere improvement is not enough; only 'transformation' will do. Incremental innovations are not worth bothering with; instead, companies urge 'breakthroughs'. . ."[68]

Take GM's approach to responding to imports — $1.9 billion was spent on a state-of-the-art new plant for the Saturn car. After taking three years to make the decision and four years to build the plant, the result is a car which at best may have a slight competitive advantage in performance and features but no advantage in cost. In contrast, during roughly the same period Honda spent $2 billion, steadily upgrading its U.S. plants as demand and the work force developed.

Honda not only sold cars as it learned how to make them more efficiently, it wound up with twice the capacity that GM has for the same cost.[69]

Looking for dramatic breakthroughs versus steadily getting better is one difference between the cultures. Another is that in Japan, everyone seems to have a strong desire to be the best at whatever they do. Once I watched a janitor in a Tokyo hotel place some cut plants in two vases hung high over a staircase. After placing the plants in each vase and carefully adjusting them just so, he walked down to the bottom of the staircase to see how they looked from that point. Not satisfied, he again put up his ladder and made another adjustment. Taking down the ladder, he checked his work again. Finally satisfied, he walked off. When I got my lower jaw in contact with my upper, all I could think of was that I would probably never see that in New York.

The Japanese culture places a high premium on dependability, concern for quality, cooperative behavior, and respect for authority.[70] Standing out as an individual is not acceptable, nor is conflict and confrontation. Also, although they have no monopoly, the citizens of both Japan and Germany seem to have a better appreciation than Americans do for the fact that if you want more, you must produce more.

Since these values are consistent with the quality culture, it is probably correct to say that the Japanese really do have a slight cultural advantage in some respects. This is not to say that the Japanese culture is ideal by any means. Indeed, the U.S. has an entrepreneurial tradition that other countries would like to copy.

Although national cultural differences and advantages do exist, there is no evidence these differences are very significant or are big obstacles. For example, when Mitsubishi established a forklift plant in Houston, it estimated the local employees would be 75 percent as productive as those in Japan. But Mitsubishi found the Yanks were every bit as good as their Japanese peers. As a result, output was quickly boosted to 400 units per month — roughly three years ahead of schedule.[71] This story has been repeated at many other companies.

Summary

Beliefs and values affect how people see the world and will react to it. There is a direct relationship between a company's culture and what it will do, what it can do, how it gets things done, and what level of performance it will achieve. The quality culture requires companies, managers, and employees to see each other and the world in a special light:

- Companies need to see their customers not as the next sale but as long term friends who derive real benefits and value from their goods or services. Companies must always be asking how they can provide more value to their customers rather than how they can collect the most money from them.
- CEOs need to see their organization as a set of meshed gears working toward a common purpose, not as isolated lines and boxes. They, along with all managers, must pay as much attention to doing the right things as they do to getting the right results.
- CEOs must see themselves as the driving force for change, innovation, and high standards of performance.
- Managers must see themselves as being primarily responsible for improving quality and productivity, instead of blaming all problems on the workers.
- Managers and supervisors must see themselves as teachers, communicators, and facilitators, not as policemen.

- Sales representatives must see themselves not just as pushers of products, but as a vital source of information about their customers' needs and wants.
- Companies must see their vendors as an extension of themselves and as long term partners with whom they must communicate and cooperate, not as adversaries to keep in the dark and off-balance.
- Companies must see their employees as their most important asset. They must realize that one of the best investments they can make is in improving the capability of their employees to contribute to the company's success. As John Mariotti says, "People have to know more if they're going to produce more."[72]
- All employees must see themselves as important parts of their companies and realize that their job security and success depends more upon their own efforts than on anything else.

These social characteristics are important because they complement the technical tools and processes needed to improve quality. Performance measurement, problem analysis, problem solving, and implementation of changes can occur in any environment, but in the quality culture, their effectiveness is maximized.

Within the framework of the quality culture, there is considerable room for adapting to different local situations. However, it must be kept in mind that the objective is to adapt the company to the quality culture, not the other way around.

CHAPTER 10

Implementation

S INCE QUALITY applies to every aspect of a business, any efforts to improve quality should address the entire company — including its suppliers. As a practical matter, resources are always limited. Trying to go too far too fast will only waste resources and may also result in lost credibility. It is perfectly acceptable, and probably necessary, to tackle only a few departments at a time. In that case, it must be made clear that ultimately everyone will be affected. *Everybody needs to be measured, everybody needs to be accountable, and everybody needs to be involved.*

Using a double standard is one sure way to fail. How can anyone expect people in one department to feel good about being asked to improve performance when they see other departments getting away with murder? Besides, as you will quickly see from the variance analysis, many of the causes of poor quality *within* a department are coming from *outside* the department.

The following steps outline an approach that can be applied to virtually any company or function within it. It is important that the steps be followed in sequence and that none of them are bypassed. There is a sound reason for each step, and there are no shortcuts to success.

This plan covers only the high points. Implementation is relatively systematic and easy in that sense, but getting to the details is not exactly a walk in the park...well, maybe Central Park at 3 A.M. Implementation can best be described as a series of concentric circles, spiraling inward toward the objective most of the time. Some problems will be solved very easily and others will make untying the Gordian Knot look like child's play. Planning is worthwhile, but getting too detailed, trying to look very far ahead, or setting rigid timetables is an exercise in futility. The ugly truth is that you won't know something will work until it does. About the only thing you can be sure of, is that anyone who tells you everything is just wonderful during implementation is either drunk or lying.

At the Company Level

Step 1: Commit to improving performance.

If you're not going to give the quality improvement program your wholehearted support and a sufficient amount of your time, don't bother to start. Aborted attempts will not be forgotten. If there is one critical ingredient in the formula for success, it is the perseverance that comes from total commitment. Waiting for the "right time" may have some merit but the best time is now. Otherwise, it may be too late.

Step 2: Sell the program to management.

Everyone must see how they are going to benefit in terms they can understand. This applies at every level in the company. Managers are no different from hourly workers. Middle managers and supervisors are most likely to feel threatened because they see a potential loss of power. They may also be the most affected by having to change their management styles.

What's going to be said should be worked out in advance. The "selling" must be in terms that are positive, factual, and logical. Explaining why is very important. Sound arguments you can use are as follows.

It is in everyone's interest:

- *For the company to be as profitable as possible.* Without profits, companies cease to exist. Profits mean benefits, good wages, and good working conditions.
- *For the company to not only survive, but also to grow.* This requires investment which must come from profits and provides opportunity for promotion, personal growth, and job security.
- *For the company to be the best in its industry,* or at least continuously striving to be the best. Besides keeping customers and making growth possible, most everyone wants to work for a great company. Pride in where you work is an important factor in self-esteem. Nobody really likes to work for a company with a less than admirable reputation.
- *For operations to run as smoothly as possible.* Although people show a remarkable ability to cope with problems, nobody likes a job filled with daily frustrations. The ultimate result of confusion and frustration is low productivity, conflict, and turnover, which affects everyone.

Step 3: Define what "productivity" and "quality" mean to your customer and your company.

The factors critical to someone else may not be meaningful to your situation and marketing strategy. No company can be all things to all people. Who are your target customers and how are you going to get their business? How do you differentiate your products and services from your competitors'? Where do you see that you can establish a competitive edge?

Answering these questions is not all that easy. It requires having knowledge and information you may not have and which you cannot quickly obtain. However, you can at least define performance parameters based on experience, knowledge of your industry and competition, and where you think you need to improve.

Any activity which doesn't contribute to the company's objectives or help it gain a competitive advantage is not productive.

Step 4: Define the key performance factors for the company.

If you know what your customer wants and you have defined a company strategy, the next step is to determine the few key success factors for the company as a whole. This might be quality levels, service factors, response times or other performance measures. Even if you can't put precise figures on acceptable limits or objectives, take your best guess. Benchmarking is certainly a preferred way of determining objectives and constraints for top level performance factors.

You must be specific and make the hard choices between conflicting variables. What you want to maximize or minimize, along with any corresponding constraints, must be clearly and operationally defined. Don't make the common mistake of asking for everything — you won't get it anyway.

Then make certain that all managers understand why these factors are important and how they relate to company objectives. Finally, make sure all managers agree with them.

Step 5: Define the performance measures and constraints for each operating unit of the company, if this has no already been accomplished during Step 4.

Each division, department, or other unit must have specific performance measures that support the company's objectives. Figure 10.1 is a form that can be used for that purpose.

Where there are conflicting objectives, evaluate the trade-offs and make an appropriate decision. Building conflict into the performance/reward system for different departments is self-defeating. Competition within a company may be helpful, but conflict is not.

DEPARTMENT PERFORMANCE DEFINITION

DEPARTMENT   *Shipping*

PRIMARY PERFORMANCE MEASURES	MINIMUM	MAXIMUM	OBJECTIVE
1. *Accuracy of orders*			*100%*
2. *% of orders shipped in 8 hrs.*	*95%*		*100%*
3.			
4.			
5.			

SECONDARY PERFORMANCE MEASURES	MINIMUM	MAXIMUM	OBJECTIVE
1. *Total cost/order shipped*			*minimize*
2. *Total cost/order shipped*			
3.			
4.			
5.			

Figure 10.1 Department Performance Measure Worksheet

*Step 6: Assign someone to be accountable
for each key performance factor*

Without single point accountability, not much will happen. This means that one person must be accountable for each performance measure, not two, three, or a committee. Where lines of responsibility are not clear, assign the performance measure to the person who has the most direct control.

At the Department and Individual Level

Step 7: Sell the program again.

The first thing you do is to start changing the way everyone thinks. Answer the question everyone will ask: "What's in it for me? It may be necessary to guarantee that people won't lose their jobs or take cuts in pay if positions are eliminated. Appealing only to the good health of the company and motherhood isn't enough.

The part of the program that will be the hardest to sell is going to be the reporting and close monitoring of performance. It will not only be seen as an added burden, but also as a potential threat — "Big Brother" is coming into our lives. The issues mentioned in Step 2 are still relevant, but other rational reasons for having to collect the data and measure performance are:

- *The CEO and other managers are already being measured by sales, profits, and other factors.* Why shouldn't everyone and everything else be measured?
- *The primary purpose for collecting the data is to measure the performance of the production system so the weaknesses can be identified and corrected.* The purpose is not to identify people who may be poor performers — those are generally well-known anyway.

Although there is no question that the information could contribute to a person's performance evaluation, (1) the information will be objective rather than subjective and (2) everyone will be measured in a similar manner. Given the choice, objective measures are preferred over someone's opinion.

Consistent with that intent, I recommend establishing a policy that no one will be punished for making a mistake (making the same one over and over is another matter), but that a person who falsifies data will be given the opportunity to work for another company. The reason for such a policy is that false data will destroy the credibility of the information and may result in wasting valuable resources and time.

After making that policy, you must stick with it. If your mind is on punishing people instead of solving problems, you might as well forget improving performance anyway. The first time you use the information to reprimand or punish someone, the game will be over and you'll be the loser.

People will not object to reporting anything if:

- They understand the purpose.
- They see the data being used for that purpose.
- They see some benefit from doing it.
- They don't see it as a threat.
- It is relatively easy to do.

Step 8: Perform the opportunity identification procedures in each department.

Since each of these methods can identify opportunities the others cannot, it is best to use all of them. Benchmarking is not necessary for getting started on quality improvement, but since it provides the only basis for comparing a company with the outside world, it should be considered mandatory at some early point.

Step 9: From the opportunity surveys determine the
information needed to measure and manage performance.

This will include both "micro" and "macro" production processes. Micro-processes are operations such as drilling holes, coating metal, or extruding plastic. This is the traditional area where SPC has been applied and where statistical tools like control charts are almost certainly required.

Macro-processes are such things as departments, functions within departments, or shifts. There is probably very little value in doing anything more than plotting a run chart for these upper-level measures. In the first place, they are typically so far removed from the actionable level that any problems will be detected there first. In the second place, these upper level measures may be affected by so many external factors that they are never really "in control" in a statistical sense.

Regardless, measuring the performance of these aggregate production systems is just as important as measuring individual manufacturing operations. The performance measures may be mostly symptomatic, but they are important for understanding how the larger processes work and for all the other reasons discussed in Chapter 3.

To determine what variables should be measured, first review each department for variables which impact the company's key performance factors. Then review the results of each analysis procedure for recurring causes of poor quality and waste. The opportunity identification procedures will also point to physical processes which need to be measured. That is where engineers and technicians will have to identify what variables are important and how they interact.

Next, rank the various quality and waste factors for each operating level in order of their cost or impact. This is to separate what's important from what's not. Typically 80 to 90 percent of a problem will be caused by something like 20 to 30 percent of the variables involved. It isn't practical to measure everything, nor is it necessary to do so. Start with the big chunks, and after you get them out of the way, some of those unimportant factors will become important. For example, in Table 10.1, we could ignore everything below cause D and we would still account for most of the problem.

Table 10.1 An Example of Ranking Variables by Importance

CAUSE	% OF PROBLEM	TOTAL
A	32	32
B	20	60
C	22	82
D	11	93
E	3	96
F	1	97
Other	3	100

Getting the numbers in Table 10.1 is called performing a Pareto analysis, which is nothing more than simply ranking importance. And while it is necessary to do the ranking so you don't waste time on small problems, why such an obvious concept deserves having anyone's name attached to it is beyond me. Mr. Pareto must have had a good press agent. If you prefer, you can plot the relative importance of each cause ("percent of problem" above) on a graph, which is called a Pareto diagram.

Even after doing all this work, you have not identified everything you need to measure — but you do have a good starting point. As you use them, you will surely learn that some measures will be meaningful, others will not, and others will be missing.

Step 10: Design a system to collect and process the data.

This does not have to be an elaborate computer system. The manual tabulation method shown by Figure 10.2 can be used in most situations, once the quality problems have been defined. A manual system, as shown by Figure 10.3, can then be used to summarize the data. Manual systems can be quite

DESCRIPTION	TALLY	COUNT
frammer glangs	JHT JHT IIII	14
zort wizzies	JHT JHT JHT JHT II	22
nerbel glotches	JHT I	6

Figure 10.2 Manual Scheme for Collecting Data

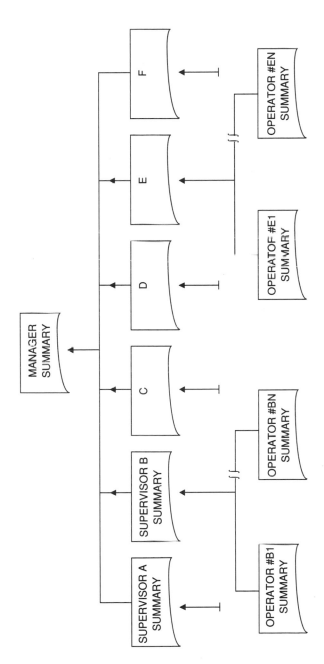

Figure 10.3 A Manual Data Collection and Processing System

efficient. In fact, there's a lot to be said for getting people involved in summarizing the data. This assures it will be reviewed and creates a sense of ownership not provided by a computer report.

Typically, much of the necessary information such as materials, labor, work inputs and outputs is already being collected by existing systems. You must make sure, however, that the information represents what you think it does and that long delays aren't built into the system.

Where manual systems are not practical, small computers can be used to advantage. There is a broad choice of cheap and effective tools readily available. The many database management programs on the market are well-suited for this purpose. A big advantage of computers is that once the data is entered, it is readily available for special analyses that might only be rarely required.

Figure 10.4 is a form used to collect data which was put into a computer for analysis. In this case, for the data to be useful it was necessary to not only identify the defect, but the model and the location of the problem as well. Collecting the data only by defect type provided some useful information, but it was often necessary to identify specific models in order to isolate the causes of problems.

Collecting and processing data is costly. For that reason you should collect only what you need, process only what you need, and only do it as often as you need. A shotgun approach will not work. Once you know what must be measured, an efficient data collection/processing system can be designed.

*Step 11: Define specifications for the identified variances
and quality factors as required.*

In some cases, the difference between "good" and "bad" quality will be obvious. In others, it will be necessary to develop both a specification and a way of measuring compliance.

UPHOLSTERY DEPARTMENT DAILY QUALITY REPORT

NAME _R. Herrin_   PLANT _3_ LINE _2_ DATE _6·2·90_

NO.	MODEL NO.	DEFECT	LOCATION	COUNT	QTY	DEFECT/LOCATION CODES
1	243-1	27	IB	⦀ 1	6	**FRAMES**
2	422-3	11	OA	‖	2	01 Leg plates
3	422-3	12	OA	∣	1	02 Spring clips missing / 03 Spring rails bowing
4	317-2	01		⫼	3	04 Staple sticking out
5						05 Splice sticking out
6						10 Rough lumber
7						11 Warped piece
8						12 Broken piece
9						13 T-nuts
10						20 Not level
11						21 Not square
12						22 Back pitch
13						23 Back alignment
14						24 Arm Alignment

Codes list (right column):

FRAMES
01 Leg plates
02 Spring clips missing
03 Spring rails bowing
04 Staple sticking out
05 Splice sticking out
10 Rough lumber
11 Warped piece
12 Broken piece
13 T-nuts
20 Not level
21 Not square
22 Back pitch
23 Back alignment
24 Arm Alignment
25 Underhang
26 Overhang
27 Buildup required
28 Hole alignment
900 Other

FABRIC		SEWING
40 Flaw		47 Pleats
41 Dirt		48 Top stitch
42 Tear		
944 Other		
45 Dimension		

FOAM
50 Dimension
51 Hard/tight
52 Soft/loose
53 Damage
955 Other
56 Poor dacron wrap

LOCATION
S,B,A Seat, Back, Arm
IB In-back
OB Out-back
IA In-arm
OA Out-arm
SC Seat Cushion
BC Back cushion
SB Seat-back
FSA Front seat-arm
BSA Back seat-arm
TAB Top arm-back

NOTES — REFER TO ITEM NUMBER ABOVE

Figure 10.4 Sample Data Collection Form

Specifications must be thorough and unambiguous. If you can't tell someone what you want, how can you expect them to provide it?

Step 12: Collect operating data for one or two weeks.

Don't start making changes to production processes. Instead, strive for consistency in operations so that you have a known point of reference. When trying to improve performance, it is better to be consistently bad than to be hopping all over the place in frantic attempts to correct weaknesses in a production process.

During this period, it is helpful to note any abnormal conditions so the data can be excluded or adjusted. Don't worry about having a highly accurate figure; 10 to 20 percent error is quite acceptable. As everyone gains experience with collecting data, the errors will quickly decrease.

From this data, determine the average value of each performance measure. This will provide a base for setting priorities and measuring progress. At this point, the ranking (Pareto) analysis should be repeated since the information will be more complete. From this, you may find new variables which should be measured and a few that should be dropped. Don't worry about having the perfect system. No matter how much effort you put into it, you will find it necessary to make changes when you start using the system.

Step 13: Using the current average figures as a guide, determine priorities for action and objectives for each measure.

Priorities must be established, because there will surely be more problems than resources available to solve them. If you've done a halfway decent job of selling the program, one of the difficulties will be keeping everyone focused on a manageable set of priorities. Some managers and supervisors will want to attack every problem at once. While their enthusiasm may be admirable, that approach is doomed to failure.

Goals may have to be purely judgmental. After all, you are going into new territory and no one really knows what is possible. Objectives should be ambitious and go beyond what everyone thinks can be done. A good starting point is to set an initial goal of cutting each quality and waste problem in half. As experience is gained, raise or lower objectives to keep them aggressive but attainable.

People want to see themselves as winners, so focus attention on only a limited number of objectives in each work group. Pick the items that seem to offer the most promise of success and work on them first. Show some positive results early and support for the program will grow.

Don't set goals for productivity or even talk about it! If you want to stop the program dead in its tracks, just announce at a meeting: "We're going to increase productivity around here." That's a great way to get everyone's support — insult them by telling them they haven't been working and then tell them they're going to have to work harder.

Talking about productivity also diverts attention from what matters. A high level of productivity is only the result of doing other things right. *The best way to increase productivity is to work on something else* — the quality and waste factors throughout the production system. Take care of the nickels and dimes and the dollars will take care of themselves.

Step 14: Assign responsibility for each of the individual performance measures throughout the system.

As stated earlier, someone must "own" each performance measure down to the lowest level of detail. There can be no orphans or children with more than one parent.

Step 15: Start taking action.

Problems can be assigned to managers and supervisors, who then can distribute them to individuals or teams. By spreading the work across a broad base, considerable progress can be made in a short period of time with no one working on more than one or two problems at a time.

Step 16: Put each performance measure on a graph
and update it on a regular basis.

Where control charts and other statistical methods are used to monitor physical processes, the frequency of measurement will be dictated by the speed and stability of the process. Although these variables will have their own charts, broader measures of quality and productivity such as percent defectives should also be measured.

Weekly updates of graphs (from daily summary reports) are usually sufficient for summary information. Putting results on neat graphs makes it easy to recognize trends and to identify problems or opportunities needing attention. This is one case where one picture is truly worth a thousand words. One performance factor per graph is recommended for clarity. Figure 6.4 is a good example to follow.

Step 17: Revise the data collection and
performance measurement system as required
to provide meaningful and timely information.

The first attempt at setting up a performance measurement system will undoubtedly be lacking in some respects. As attempts are made to identify and solve problems, you will discover additional detail is needed to get down to their root causes. Also, as the larger problems are solved, more problems will become apparent and important. What starts out as twenty variables may well end up as sixty.

Check to see what information is being used. If anything is not being used, it is probably because it is not telling the users what they need to know. In that case, don't blindly defend the system, change it until it is correct.

One of the surest signs the system is being used is that changes are being made to it. Most of these changes will occur in the first several months of operation. After that, relatively few changes will be required. However, even after a few years of use, changes will be necessary from time to time. As a business changes, so must the information to manage it.

Summary

The first step in improving quality is to start changing a company's culture. This obviously cannot be done in a few days, but some groundwork must be laid so that everyone understands what is going to happen, why, and how it affects them. Even with a well-planned and executed effort, not everyone will buy into the program at first. It takes constant repetition and demonstration to change the way people think. In reality, building the right culture never ends, just as improving performance never ends.

Implementing a performance measurement system is not a cut and dried proposition, but it doesn't require managers to be technical wizards or dynamic leaders either. For the most part, it can be approached methodically using the given procedures.

The key to developing an efficient and effective measurement system is to use it. As it is used, weaknesses and voids will be discovered which must be corrected. Like any other learning experience, developing a performance measurement system is a process of trial and error to some degree. The longer it is used, the more valuable it becomes, along with the organization using it.

CHAPTER 11

Managing Performance

PERFORMANCE measures will produce few benefits by themselves. Better performance can only come from improving the production processes within a company. Making the decisions and taking the necessary actions to accomplish that is primarily a process of communicating and learning. The following steps provide a guide for using performance measures effectively to manage and improve performance. Many details of what to say and do will have to be supplied by the user, but the basics are certainly not very complicated.

1. Give every manager a set of performance graphs for his or her area of responsibility on a timely basis.

Generally, this means weekly, and within one working day after the week ends. If the week ends Friday, the graphs should be distributed by noon on Monday at the latest. Each manager or department head should get only the graphs related to his or her area of responsibility. Besides saving paper, this spells out accountability in very clear terms. This does not mean, however, that access to any other relevant information should be restricted. It can be included, but it should be clearly separated from the core information.

Bear in mind that the weekly update requirement is for summary information only. There will be more frequent reports and graphs that reach all the way down to the actionable level. To make good decisions, it is necessary to be able to see both the big picture and the details. A typical hierarchy of information might look like this:

- TOTAL REJECTS (weekly graph)
  - Rejects by reason (weekly graph)
    - Rejects by machine and reason (daily report)
      - Control charts for each machine, measured as required

There should also be daily and weekly reports for the department as a whole, summarizing quality, productivity, waste and other measures. *The objective is for every manager, from the foreman or department supervisor on up, to have a good understanding of what happened each day and each week.* At the operator level, by recording and reviewing data, operators will be keeping a real-time record and will know what has happened up to any point in time.

2. Display in each department the graphs of that department's key performance factors.

Make every department's performance visible. There is nothing wrong with having problems and pretending you don't have them surely won't solve them. Bringing all the problems to the surface and making someone accountable for each of them seems threatening, but it is actually refreshing. It clears the air and establishes a constructive atmosphere where everyone can admit their mistakes and problems like adults, instead of covering them up and acting like defensive children. Pretending there are no problems and pointing fingers are exercises which have been raised to a fine art by politicians, but that is no way to run a business.

Making everyone's performance visible has some subtle and powerful effects. First, everyone can take pride in what they have accomplished. Second, where nothing has been accomplished, hanging the dirty laundry out for everyone to see will create peer pressure to meet group objectives. Those who haven't been contributing will probably receive comments from their co-workers, which can have a much greater impact than the same words from management. The same applies equally well to managers at all levels.

Displaying performance also reinforces a feeling of teamwork by letting everyone see how other groups are contributing to common goals. It answers the question: "We're busting our buns in department X; what are those turkeys in department Y doing?"

For this reason, graphs of the key factors for all the departments should be posted where everyone can see them. Creating a "War Room" for displaying all the key measures of the company and departments is an effective approach. In a few instances, it may be necessary to disguise sensitive information by using a relative index, but this usually isn't a big problem.

Remember what was said about anxiety and the need to see a difference between where you are and where you want to be? The graphs will provide a constant reminder that additional improvements in performance are possible — at least until everything is perfect. Improving quality is a never-ending process and the graphs will help get that point across.

3. Use the information to identify problems, ask questions, recognize performance, make decisions, and take action.

Graphs and reports are important, but the objective is not to cover the walls with expensive wallpaper. If it is not used effectively, information is just another form of waste. With good timely information, managers can ask specific questions of specific people. Some of the best are:

- "I see xxxx was up/down last week. What caused it?"
- "What do you think the problem is?"
- "What do think might solve it?"
- "What is being done about it?"
- "What are (your, your department's, your group's) priorities?"

Review summary reports each day to identify any large variations in performance which need immediate attention. Asking questions similar to those above will tell you if they have already been addressed by the people closest to the problem. When you ask them, see if you get reasons, guesses, excuses, or an "I don't know" as an answer. Remember, understanding the behavior of the production system is perhaps the most important reason for measuring performance.

Hold frequent brief mini-meetings to discuss problems, possible solutions, and plans for action. At the department or work group level, a ten-minute meeting at the end of each day to review what went wrong and what went right that day can be very effective. In my opinion, this is one of the best ways to get useful information and suggestions. This may be "idle" time in the working sense, but it is certainly very productive time with respect to improving quality.

Every week, hold a meeting with all department heads to review: (1) decisions made, (2) actions taken, (3) results achieved, (4) problems solved, (5) any new problems discovered, and (6) what resources or assistance would be helpful. Priorities for each department, group, or person also need to be reviewed and revised as appropriate, being careful not to give people more than they can reasonably handle. Having too many "Number One Priorities" will only lead to confusion and frustration.

Voluntary teams need much the same treatment, but they also need the freedom to work on projects that they select. However, when they understand the current priorities for the company and department, it is unlikely they will want to deviate too far from the priorities anyway. In the long run, it doesn't make much difference if a team chooses to work on Priority 10 when working on Priority 5 might be better. It is worthwhile effort in any case. Besides, any estimate of priorities is not necessarily all that accurate to begin with.

Don't just use the information for managing the mechanics. Use it to recognize and reward accomplishment also! Public and one-on-one praise will go a long way toward getting everyone enthused and involved. Some of the best words to use are simply "Thank you for your help."

Celebrate small successes with small rewards. Small unexpected rewards can be more effective than large expected rewards. Just give someone a small present when it is not a normal occasion for such behavior and see what happens! When some noticeable progress has been made, buy everyone lunch, pass out candy, or let everyone go home an hour early on Friday (with pay). The possibilities are endless and inexpensive. Improving performance can be real drudgery at times, but it can also be fun. Nobody ever said you can't talk, laugh, and work hard at the same time.

One note of caution. While it is important to recognize individuals, be wary of creating superstars. Spread the glory around and emphasize group achievement more than individual effort. If you appear to favor a few individuals, those not included will feel left out and alienated. That is one of the potential problems with Quality Circles.[73]

In meetings, ask everyone to contribute. Initially, only a few people will actively participate, but as time passes, fears and inhibitions will subside. With some encouragement, most of the quiet people in the back row will eventually come around and be an active part of the team. Even if they don't, they won't be able to say they weren't given the chance to be heard.

Recognizing someone who tries and fails is as important as recognizing those who succeed. Chastise people for failing and they will quickly learn to quit trying. Criticize them for offering impractical suggestions and they will learn to be quiet. Negative feedback is occasionally needed, but 90 percent of the feedback in business is negative[74] — which is way too much. Emphasize the positive aspects of effort as well as results.

Take a lesson from Harry Quadracci, CEO of Quad/Graphics. When a division spent three years and $1 million developing a new folder that didn't work, he threw a champagne party and awarded a medal to the project leader! He says he can't imagine reprimanding employees, let alone firing them, for taking risks that fail.[75] Of course, not all behavior or failure is acceptable, but honest efforts should be recognized. Managers who are not perfect certainly have no right to criticize others for not being right all the time.

Don't use false praise, however. It will quickly be seen for what it is. Maintaining credibility is important. There is only one way to play the game and that is to play it straight. Being tactful doesn't hurt, but don't confuse that with being truthful. *The One-Minute Manager* is a good model to follow for giving feedback about performance. Feedback should be frequent so learning can take place. A fifteen-minute "performance review" once a year is woefully inadequate for anyone to learn to do anything better.

4. Use the Scientific Method to diagnose problems and test solutions.

Ask yourself how you know that your diagnosis of the problem is correct. What would you say if someone asked you, "How do you know that what you say is so?"

- Are you acting on emotion or do you have some evidence to support your conclusion?
- Do the facts support your theory of what is causing the problem?
- If you have diagnosed the problem correctly and have a good solution, what are the expected results? Did you get them?

Solving problems and taking advantage of opportunities requires logical analysis, creative thinking, and a great deal of trial and error. Most learning occurs because of failure, and improving the performance of any production system is very much a learning process.

Above everything else, *do something* — but only after you have thought the problem through and feel you are on the right track. Don't get analysis paralysis and be afraid to make a move for fear it won't work. If you can't pin down the cause of a problem, set up an experiment or collect more detailed data which may provide clues to the puzzle. If your idea turns out be as useful as a lead life preserver, at least you'll have learned something and can take the next step that much sooner. *The only people who never fail are those who never try anything.*

Every manager would like to hear otherwise, but the truth of the matter is that patiently solving one problem after another is the only way to improve quality and productivity. Luck does happen, but not often. By developing potential solutions, testing them, and going back to the drawing board as many times as necessary, any problem can be solved.

5. Keep everyone informed on progress and new developments.

Everyone needs to be kept up-to-date about accomplishments, the current state of affairs, and the outlook for the future. Besides being good for morale, it gives everyone a common frame of reference for setting priorities and making decisions.

Employees want to know what their company is doing. If they don't know, it certainly isn't "their" company. In a very real sense, employees are the customers of management and they have a right to know about decisions being made which may affect them. Of course, some strategic information can't be disclosed, but that is not an excuse for keeping everyone in the dark.

Periodic meetings are also opportunities for top management to sell the concept of continuous quality improvement. Since it will take many words and actions to change the way everyone thinks, opportunities to send the message should not be missed. Certainly some hype and fanfare are appropriate, but it is my experience that people are more interested in hard facts and substance than in superficial puffery. Improving quality and changing a company's culture is not a motivational trick. If employees start to see it as a game, the game is over.

6. Continually revise priorities and goals as progress is achieved.

There will always be areas for improvement and new problems occurring as products and processes change. You can always get better, and performance measures give you the ability to see where that can happen. Every month, step back and take a broader view of each performance measure and of each department as a whole.

- What are the performance measures telling you? What looks like it will break down next?
- If performance has leveled off in an area is it because there have been no attempts to improve it? Or is it because the limits of present methods have been reached? If repeated attempts to improve performance have failed, you may be trying to squeeze blood out of rocks. It may be time to look for an entirely new method.

- Where do goals need to be revised? Continuous improvement means that when goals have been achieved, new goals must be set. It may also be appropriate to back off on some objectives if it is clear that the limits of the current process have been reached. Planning is also a continuous process. There is nothing wrong with changing plans when new information becomes available. However, there is a great deal wrong with simply giving up.
- How do different departments/shifts/divisions compare? Are there good reasons for the differences? What can be learned from those doing the best in any area?
- Which departments/shifts/divisions are making gains and which ones need assistance? Where does the organization need strengthening through additional training, manpower, or other resources?
- What are the limiting factors in the production process as a whole? Where are the bottlenecks?
- What do the graphs tell you about the capacity limits of the departments? Do quality problems noticeably increase as output goes above a certain level? When that happens, it is a sign that the practical capacity of the department is being exceeded.

These and other questions must be asked continuously. Regularly reviewing, questioning, and acting on the information must become a way of life. Quality and productivity should be on everyone's mind every day, not just before each department meeting.

At the company level, the same questions must be asked. Quarterly and annual reviews *should be held to revise plans and priorities as required. The purpose of a "performance review" should be to objectively assess what has been accomplished and what should be done from that point forward, not to identify heroes or bums.* Staying objective within a company is extremely difficult under the best conditions, but in an atmosphere where managers feel they are going to be accused, punished, or rewarded, you can forget about hearing complete and unbiased information.

Managing Vendors

This topic is too complex to go into very much detail, but the principles of quality improvement that apply inside a company apply to its external suppliers as well.

The first requirement for managing vendors is to know what you want and clearly communicate it to them. As mentioned before, this is best accomplished through mutual understanding of a customer's needs and the vendors' capabilities. If suppliers are truly an extension of a company, it follows that the communications between a company and its suppliers should be on a par with what happens between internal departments. Yet, most customer-vendor relationships essentially amount to: "Here's what we make. Do you want to buy it?"

Reducing the number of vendors simplifies the communications and management problem. Xerox reduced their suppliers from 5,000 to 400, trained them, included them in the design of products, and provided functional specifications instead of detailed blueprints to give their vendors maximum freedom to satisfy Xerox's needs. As a result, from 1981 to 1984, net product costs decreased about 10 percent per year, rejects decreased by 93 percent, and both product development costs and development time decreased 50 percent.[76] This also illustrates the Law of Requisite Variety at work. It is a lot easier to manage 400 vendors than 5,000.

Managing vendors is also a learning process. For them to learn, performance information must be fed back to them on a timely and regular basis. However, from most customers, the only information a vendor receives is intermittent complaints about severe problems or those which result in rejects and returns. Even then, the information may pass through accounting channels and never get to the people who could do something to eliminate the problem.

Simply providing regular reports to vendors about delivery performance and specific quality problems can make a big difference. For example, one furniture company which was having problems with the consistency of foam cushioning discovered it was being shipped second grade material because it never complained. One factual quality report to the vendor and the practice quickly stopped.

Some companies regularly provide their vendors with a blind ranking of where they stand on various quality and service factors. That will certainly create a little anxiety! However, reports alone will never be enough for developing good understanding and relationships. The interface between a company and its suppliers is far too complex for that. On-site visits, joint development of products, linking management information systems, and forming cross-functional problem-solving teams are some of the techniques used by companies to dissolve artificial barriers and form cooperative relationships with their suppliers.

As in solving other problems, a company should not start pointing fingers at their vendors until the causes of problems have been identified. Quality problems could come from an infinite number of sources — poor specifications, unreasonable requests for delivery, poor communications, and demanding a ridiculously low price, to name a few. Hewlett-Packard, for example, found that poor communications was the root cause of most of its "vendor delivery" problems and that Hewlett-Packard was most of the problem.[77]

The quality of products coming out of a production process is limited by the quality of materials and components that are fed into it. Quality products from vendors can only come from consistent, meaningful, timely feedback and close relationships between companies and their suppliers.

Performance Standards

Performance standards have two primary uses — for evaluating performance in the good/bad sense and for planning. The only definition of a "performance standard" that makes any sense in the real world is that it represents what an average qualified person, machine, or group can accomplish under normal operating conditions. Anything more is wishful thinking; anything less is fooling yourself.

Perhaps the best way to establish an individual performance standard is to take a few people who are known to be good workers and monitor their performance closely for a day or two. By correcting the data for any unusual circumstances that may have occurred, reasonably accurate productivity and quality figures can be established.

An alternative method is to derive a standard from the performance data supplied by the performance measurement system. In this case, only data from representative sources should be included — what beginners and superstars can do is not relevant. There will always be some variation in performance between people doing the same task because of training, experience, or their natural abilities. Although an average figure can be used as a performance standard, it must be recognized that there will be variation about the average that is not necessarily either "good" or "bad."[78]

In any case, some subjective judgment must be made about the performance level of both individuals and groups. Individual standards could easily have a variation in the order of 10 percent, so they should not be thought of as absolute numbers. Where tasks are paced by machines, the figures may be more accurate, but not necessarily so. Also, translating individual standards into what can be expected from a group can be dangerous. For example, as a result of turnover, most people in a group may not yet be capable of meeting the standard.

Any standard carries with it assumed conditions. Unless the standard conditions exist, the performance standard is meaningless. Since "standard conditions" are not always satisfied, when actual performance differs significantly from the standard, it is necessary to determine whether or not (1) the standard is wrong, (2) the conditions were not satisfied, or (3) the deviation from the standard was due solely to performance. Standards must be clearly understood and constantly verified. Only then will they be a valid reference for planning and for evaluating performance.

Planning standards can sometimes be different from performance standards. The best standard to use for planning is usually what happened in the past, but there may be a valid reason for using something else. However, it is not unusual to see plans and budgets prepared using performance figures that have never been achieved and probably never will be. If someone pays attention to them, performance measures can greatly improve the quality of plans and budgets.

The most important thing to keep in mind about performance standards is *that they only define expected performance using current methods and procedures. As such, they should be thought of as minimum acceptable levels of performance, not the best that can be achieved.* When people equate "standard" with "the best," the desire to improve performance vanishes when the standard is reached. There should always be a difference between current performance and objectives, otherwise there is no reason to improve.

Summary

Communicating and learning are the key elements of managing performance. The primary steps are analyzing information, setting priorities, formulating solutions to problems,

taking action, and checking the results. Interwoven throughout this process are recognition, reward, teaching, and learning. Managing performance focuses on explaining and
narrowing the gap between actual and desired performance.
The fundamental steps involved are not complicated, but
identifying problems and developing solutions is frequently a
difficult process. By continuously reviewing the information,
asking good questions, seeking solutions, and taking action,
success may not come easily, but it will come.

It is true that you can always get better, but it is also true
that any machine or system has its limits. When these limits
are reached, it is time to look at changing basic methods in
the production system which can take performance to a new
plateau. While performance measures will not tell you what
to do, they will indicate when and where fundamental
changes are needed in a production process.

CHAPTER 12

Applications

M ENTION quality and productivity and an image of a production line flashes through almost everyone's mind, but there are quality and productivity dimensions to any business activity. Blue-collar productivity is certainly important, but the facts are that: (1) on a national basis, white-collar workers outnumber blue-collar workers; (2) white-collar workers account for an even greater portion of wages; and (3) white-collar workers have a greater impact on a company's total performance than do blue- collar workers.

Even for manufacturing companies, it is rare for direct labor costs to exceed 15 percent of production costs.[79] It is also true that white-collar performance can have a dramatic effect on blue-collar quality and productivity. *In fact, low blue-collar productivity is a result of poor white-collar performance.* After all, who else is responsible for the blue-collar workers and their production systems? Managers looking for someone to blame for poor blue-collar performance should first look into a mirror. As Pogo Possum said, "We have met the enemy and they is us."[80]

Regardless, *no matter what color someone's collar is, their performance is important to a business and it should be measured.*

Companies need to become as concerned about white-collar performance as they are about blue-collar performance. Quality and productivity don't stop at the plant door, yet companies that measure the productivity of their $10/hour line employees with pinpoint accuracy are likely to have no idea of how well their entire engineering department is performing.[81]

A few interesting statistics about white collar work:

1. About 20 percent of all white-collar work involves correcting errors.
2. Another 20 percent of all white-collar work involves preventing errors that should have been designed out of the production process.
3. Another 10 percent of all white-collar work is ineffective, unnecessary, or optional.[82]

By 1995, indirect labor is expected to account for over 80 percent of the work force. Yet, only about 5 percent of white-collar and service-sector employees are subject to some form of work measurement. An analysis of these unmeasured, non-production workers has shown that they rarely exceed 60-percent efficiency.[83]

Peter Drucker maintains that for the rest of this century — and far into the next one — the competitive battle will be won or lost by white-collar productivity because some countries have such an advantage in low cost labor that those with advanced economies cannot compete solely on a labor cost basis.[84] Based on the hard evidence of jobs lost to developing countries, it is difficult to argue with that position. The question is whether or not companies in more advanced countries like the U.S. are going to start doing something about it. The way to start is to forget about artificial distinctions based on the color of shirts and start measuring everyone's performance.

The methods and procedures given here can be applied to any recurring activity. This would include nearly every business function because, like problems, most business activities are recurring. Placing advertising, preparing financial reports, and typing memos are easily recognizable as repetitive operations, but even jobs that repeat infrequently can be measured, analyzed, and improved.

For instance, preflight tests of missiles occurred only a handful of times each year, but the time to conduct them was significantly reduced using these methods. After identifying the reasons for delays and idle time, specifications and clear-cut lines of responsibility were defined for each phase of the tests. Then, the causes of poor quality throughout the process were corrected. Procedures were rewritten, cables and equipment were clearly labeled, and equipment deficiencies were corrected. After a few cycles to get the bugs out, tests that used to take four hours were taking only two. In addition, everyone involved in the tests was much happier with the way things ran. On a scale of 1 to 10, aggravation dropped from 9.9 to about 0.1.

As long as the activities are recurring, the principles can be applied. It makes no difference how frequently they are repeated.

Measuring White-collar Performance

Apparently there are three reasons (none of them good) for not measuring the performance of white-collar business functions. The first is that the value of doing it is not recognized. Hopefully, this book will have successfully argued that point by now.

The second is that it is generally assumed most white-collar activities cannot be measured. This is an excuse, not a reason. The big obstacle to measuring white-collar performance is defining exactly what a department is supposed to accomplish. Typically, administrative functions are defined in terms of activities instead of outputs or products. Identifying the product is the key to measuring any function.

For example, a customer service department takes calls and answers letters, but the end product is supposed to be a satisfied customer. How do you measure satisfied customers? Well, you can do surveys for one thing. Other relative indicators might be the number of customers who have to call more than once, the number of complaints that result in a return, and even the number of nasty letters received by the president of the company.

Certainly most white-collar functions are necessary or beneficial, but they should exist only to perform specific tasks or accomplish specific objectives. In that case, they should be providing a useful output to a customer. Since white-collar activities consume measurable resources, it must be possible to develop ratios and other measures which are indicators of performance. Just because a department's purpose and performance measures haven't been defined doesn't mean that it can't be done.

No department should ever just "do,"
it should always do with a specific purpose.

No one can tell you how to measure engineering, accounting, or any other generic function any more than one universal set of factors can apply to every manufacturing operation. But if you take a specific function in a company and talk to its customers about their needs, their wants, and the problems they experience, useful measures and indicators can be identified. Virtually any department producing a useful output can be measured in one way or another. Many so-called "overhead" departments are essentially no different from manufacturing departments, performing fairly repetitive and measurable tasks. Others can be measured by other means as illustrated by the examples given earlier. (See Figure 5.2.)

The point is not that any single number has any meaning by itself, but that consistent measurement will identify trends and shifts that are meaningful and valuable indicators. It doesn't matter if the measurements are not absolute based on some international standard. If the performance measures reflect the primary functions of the department and its customers' needs, they will greatly improve management's ability to improve performance. *The theory that white-collar performance cannot be measured in a meaningful way does not hold up on close examination. What is lacking is not the means but the will to do it.*

The third, and worst, reason for not measuring white-collar performance is that white-collar managers generally have the luxury of excusing themselves from being held accountable for performance. On the other hand, managers want to have clear performance goals, be measured objectively, and have their pay clearly tied to performance. You can't have it both ways. Managers who feel threatened by the concept of performance measurement must realize the advantages outweigh the disadvantages by a wide margin — for both them and their company.

Continental Insurance illustrates how performance measurement can affect managers' attitudes as well as operating performance in a typical administrative environment. Observing wide variations in costs in its branch offices, the company commissioned a study which showed that about half of the variation was caused by productivity differences and the other half by differences in activities in the offices.

This led to developing a productivity index which accounted for the differences in the various types of transactions the branches had to process. The formula for the index was fairly complex, but since the calculations were built into the data processing system, producing the information was not an expensive proposition.

The results were impressive. From 1980 to 1982, the number of employees in the branch offices decreased from 7,000 to

5,500 while service improved. Managers liked the performance measurement system, primarily for two reasons. First, it gave them a vehicle to see how they were doing — something they never had before. Second, it also provided them with an objective way to respond to pressure to improve performance. In other words, it enabled them to provide factual explanations for what was happening. Without the system, any reasons, however valid, could be dismissed by their superiors as an excuse.[85]

Again, the system wasn't perfect, but since it did account for the variables which created most of the work load, the index was a valid measure of productivity. The driving force for costs in this case was the number and type of transactions. Transactions are the key driving element in almost any white-collar function. Identifying the kinds of transactions and what causes them is the place to start looking for both opportunities and what variables should be measured.

Every transaction of materials, information, or paper uses resources. Every line item of an invoice or a health insurance form costs something to process, but most white-collar departments fail to have even the crudest measures of work input, let alone of productivity and quality. Administrative functions are typically viewed as necessary consumers of money that seem to have a growth rate of their own — a perception that is true when no one takes the time to find out what a department should be producing, what it is producing, and why. Administrative departments often accumulate unnecessary fat simply because management is not aware that there is a real cost attached to that extra report, form, or task that someone wants performed for a questionable reason.

Control transactions and you will control administrative costs to a large extent. Measure performance and use the information effectively and you will reduce and control costs even more. *The best way to eliminate a bloated administrative bu-*

reaucracy that is very busy but not productive is to prevent it from getting that way in the first place. Performance measures provide management with the ability to ask the hard questions that will nip unnecessary growth in the bud.

Measuring Sales Performance

One of the areas where productivity has tremendous leverage is in sales. Selling is viewed by most companies as an art rather than a production process. Granted, selling is not a purely mechanical exercise, but sales departments are supposed to produce qualified prospects, sales calls, and orders as the result of a great many activities. Selling may be an art, but it is also a production process where the concepts of quality and productivity apply just as well as they do to the factory making the products being sold.

Interestingly, marketing and sales costs average 15 to 35 percent of total corporate costs — a much higher percentage than direct labor.[86] More importantly, improving marketing and sales productivity not only decreases costs, it also increases revenue. When that happens, profit margins expand, so a 10 percent increase in sales as a result of better sales productivity may mean a 20 to 30 percent increase in profits. That is not exactly shabby.

What does productivity mean in terms of sales? One aspect is increasing the percentage of time the salesperson spends in contact with the customer, which usually ranges from 25 to 40 percent of his or her total work time. Another is getting the salesperson in front of the right person at the right time. Still another is allocating sales resources in proportion to the value of the account or potential value of the prospect — something that lends itself well to quantitative measures.

All of these aspects of sales productivity, and more, could be improved following the same principles and procedures that would be used in manufacturing. Again, it is a question of measuring and improving the process, not just focusing on the result.

Measuring Service Industries

Service industries are not all that different from manufacturing or administrative functions, except that the customer's expectations enter the picture. Delivering a service that meets internal standards is not sufficient if the customer's expectations have been raised beyond what can be delivered.

It is also not sufficient just to provide the service; *how* it is delivered is also important. In other words, services must be concerned not just with the outcome, but also with the process of delivery.[87]

Because both expectations and how a service was delivered can affect the customer's perceptions about a service, measuring technical completion of the service is not enough. Satisfaction must also measured, which is probably best accomplished by a survey. Other measures such as customer repeat frequency can also be reliable indicators of service quality, but may not be timely. Where surveys are concerned, statistical sampling methods can be very effective in reducing costs by reducing the number of samples required to produce reliable information.

A Note for Department Managers

Ideally, improving performance starts with the CEO and top management determining a strategy, defining key performance factors which reflect the strategy, and leading the charge to improve quality throughout the business. Unfortunately, asking for everything and changing priorities every week will continue to be standard practice in many companies. However, even in these situations, the methods and procedures given here can be used to great advantage by an individual manager or supervisor.

In the first place, most of the opportunity identification methods described earlier can be used to determine where performance can be improved. This information can be used not only to improve a department's performance but also to get proper support from other departments. For example, if another department's poor performance is causing problems for your department, it is far more likely something will be done about it if you are armed with hard facts instead of just verbal complaints. Even if you don't get what you need, at least you'll be in a good position to explain your situation.

It is also very practical to implement a good performance measurement system on a departmental basis. There is no need to wait for someone else to do it, just do it yourself. Look at the inputs, outputs, variances, waste, and other measures which are important to your department. No exotic equations or complex computer systems are required to get a pretty good understanding of the internal and external variables which affect your department. It will take a few months to get your system running smoothly, but the effort will be well worth it.

All the benefits of better understanding, control, delegation, motivation, and improved quality and productivity can be achieved at the department level by using performance measures. The performance information will also be invaluable for getting your "suppliers" in line, helping you get the resources you need, and assuring your own achievements will be recognized. Tactful use of the information with superiors can also force them to recognize that some performance measures are more important than others.

It is best for a company to approach improving performance as an integrated effort, but when that is not possible, implementing performance measurement systems on a piecemeal basis is far better than doing nothing. Managers who do so will find they have improved their own personal productivity while making their jobs easier. As a side effect, their success may just be enough to convince the entire company to do the same.

Broader Applications

Performance measurement has many benefits, whether it is applied to an isolated manufacturing process or to larger production processes such as the operation of departments or even a company. At the company level, a "Management P & L" would be an indicator of whether or not management was doing the right things which would eventually lead to getting good bottom line results. This annual report would measure such items as:

- The number of improvements made to existing products. ("Number" is used for simplicity, but ratios would also be important for most variables.)
- The number of new products brought to market and the success ratio.
- The percentage of products currently being sold that are less than 1, 3, and 5 years old.
- The number of customers gained or lost.
- The number of improvements made to internal operations.
- The number of departments that improved their performance.
- The number of employees, including managers, who improved their capabilities.
- The investment made in training as a percentage of total payroll costs. This includes direct costs and the costs of non-working time.
- The number of suggestions received from employees and the percentage implemented.
- The number of direct management contacts made with your customers and vendors.

- The relative ranking of your product and service quality as compared to your competitors' and any changes in that ranking.
- The rate of increase in your company's sales compared to the growth rate of its industry.

This partial list of measures would provide a meaningful index of how well management was doing. Even the process of quality improvement could be measured by such factors as the number of problems identified, the number of improvements made to processes, the number of quality improvement teams formed, and the hours spent on improving performance as opposed to just working on day-to-day activities. These figures would not appear on a conventional income statement, but they would be good indicators of what future income statements might look like.

Performance measurement can be applied to any endeavor. The practicality and value of measuring performance in education was demonstrated in Connecticut when it established statewide tests of competence in basic reading, writing, and arithmetic skills. As a result of the tests, school officials in Bloomfield found out in 1986 that their fourth and sixth graders were well below the average in writing. This stimulated action which produced tangible improvement. In 1986, Bloomfield was below the state average on seven of nine tests, but in 1989, it was below average on only three.[88]

The measures of competence used weren't necessarily perfect or extremely accurate, but they were capable of indicating where the job wasn't being done and rousing parents, teachers, and the school board to address the problems. Part of the testing system is to keep everyone affected well-informed. In addition to reporting the results directly to the parents and school officials, the results are published in the newspapers, creating a strong incentive for school officials to not have a poor showing.[89]

It is worthwhile to note that in this case the frequency of measurement is every other year, beginning early in a child's education. Maybe testing every year would be better, maybe not. But measuring the process in the early stages of producing the product — an educated person — is vitally important. As in making a physical product, the earlier problems are found, the easier and less costly they are to correct.

Effective use of performance measures can produce similar results in almost any business activity. The measures must be relevant, complete, understood, and accepted by everyone involved. At the same time, they don't necessarily have to be absolute or highly accurate to focus attention and resources where they are needed.

Limitations

As powerful as performance measurement can be, it is only a tool for managers to use. Like any tool, it can be used correctly or not: it is possible to play as many games with performance measures as it is with financial figures. Even if all the right measures are in place, it is entirely possible to ignore what they are telling you or to make bad decisions. Using performance measures to improve quality and productivity is not an automatic process in even the simplest cases. It takes skill, judgment, experience, and integrity to both develop and use a performance measurement system effectively.

Even when used in the best possible manner, performance measurement is certainly not the answer to all problems. *You cannot measure your way to success.* No matter how exotic or thorough the measures may be, the most they can tell you is how well you are doing, when and where problems exist, and their relative importance. They won't always tell you what is causing the problems, what will solve them, what level of performance is acceptable, or what quality factors are most important in your product or service.

Performance measures are also no substitute for managing people. To the contrary, effective use of performance measures requires managers to spend more of their time training, developing, and communicating with their employees. If used properly, performance measures can greatly enhance a manager's ability to develop individuals and an organization, but numbers in any form will never be a substitute for competent managers.

Summary

The methods and procedures given in this book can be used in any business activity to continuously improve performance. Performance measurement, problem solving, and process improvement are universally applicable disciplines which provide the same potential benefits to both white-collar and blue-collar activities.

White-collar performance is becoming increasingly important to a company's success. On balance, it deserves more attention than blue-collar performance, but it does not get the attention it should from either a general management or performance measurement perspective. Although measurement techniques may vary considerably between companies and departments, there is ample evidence to indicate that measuring white-collar performance can be done and will provide significant benefits to managers and workers as well as their companies.

However, performance measurement in any form must not be interpreted as "scientific management" or "management by the numbers." It only gives managers better information for making decisions and communicating with their fellow employees up, down, and across the organization. It is a powerful technical discipline, but it will only be effective when managers use it correctly within the right social culture.

An Overview

I MPROVING productivity and quality is not a mysterious or highly technical process. Neither is it a nicely defined problem that can be solved by a quick fix. However, it can be approached systematically using the given methods and procedures.

Working harder and investing in new equipment can be part of the solution to increased productivity and quality, but working smarter and getting all you can out of the equipment already in place should be tried first. While some innovation and creative problem solving is required, what is achieved is more a product of commitment, thoroughness, and perseverance, than of intellectual brilliance and scientific breakthroughs.

Although executing the details makes the difference between success and failure, it is helpful to step back and take a broader view of the conditions necessary for a business to achieve and maintain a high level of performance:

- *A well-defined strategy and a strong sense of purpose for competing for its chosen customers in the marketplace.*

"Strategy" doesn't mean an intricate plan. It means having a clear understanding of what you're going to be good at doing. Without that focus, being highly productive in the broad sense is impossible.

- *A commitment to continuous improvement,* focusing on the quality improvement process and long term objectives, instead of on just short term gains. If you are standing still while everyone else is moving forward, you're moving backward.
- *Leadership,* in terms of top management defining values, setting goals, and convincing everyone that improving the company's performance is in their own interest. Change must start at the top, not the bottom.
- *Total company involvement.* Quality and productivity apply to every aspect of a business and every function and department must participate in improving performance.
- *Performance measurement throughout the company,* reflecting the company's strategy and going down to the actionable level of every production process.
- *Personal identification with the company.* Everyone must understand how their company works, how they contribute, and how they will benefit from its success.
- *Decentralized management and decision-making,* putting decisions as close to the action as possible. This must also be accompanied by personal accountability for results and empowerment with the freedom and authority to achieve them.
- *Effective communication up and down the organization.* This means getting employees involved and that managers listen to them *before* decisions are made, not just afterward in order to defend the decisions. The quality of any decision is limited by the information available when it is made.

- *Close working relationships and effective two-way communications with both customers and vendors,* who are extensions of a company, not isolated entities.
- *A culture that is oriented toward change, action, and taking reasonable risks.* This requires an environment where people are not afraid to either disagree or fail.
- *Recognition and reward for behavior, effort, and achievement* which either enhances the quality improvement process or progress toward the company's objectives.
- *A skilled work force from top to bottom.* What people can conccive and do is limited by what they have experienced and learned. Training and learning must never stop.[90]

In spite of every manager's fondest wishes, there are no simple solutions or magic potions that will painlessly improve a company's performance overnight. The principles are always the same, but that doesn't mean success can be achieved by simply copying what someone else has done. Although you can learn from others, you will still have to find much of your own way, at your own pace, and develop your own solutions which are consistent with your customers, your suppliers, and your resources.

Concepts such as Just-In-Time, Material Requirements Planning, Cellular Manufacturing, and all the other currently popular management techniques have considerable merit and valid applications. For that matter, all those that have faded from memory like Management By Objectives and Transactional Analysis are still useful ways of looking at the world and addressing specific problems. All of these techniques are potentially part of the solution, but none of them is the whole solution.

In order to use any concepts or techniques effectively, you must first understand who your customers are, what they want, your competitors' capabilities, where you are, where you want to go, and the obstacles that stand in your way. Without this knowledge, you may very well end up doing the wrong things or not all the right things. There is no question that is why so many programs to make dramatic improvements in performance have failed in the past and will fail in the future.

Of course, the answers to these questions are not that easy to get and the world does not stay the same for very long. For that reason, constantly moving toward a shifting target in small steps makes a lot more sense than taking giant leaps which may be in the wrong direction.

Increasing quality and productivity is a continuous process of strengthening the weakest link. It is not a matter of overnight transformation, but of making a little progress week after week. Not everything will work the first time, but with perseverance, any problem can be solved and ambitious goals will always be reached. Patiently grinding it out isn't very dramatic, but it works.

Never stop trying to get better and never give up, but most of all, get started. The quest for quality and productivity is like going through a maze where each corridor leads to more doorways. You can only see so far ahead, but if you let that stop you, you will never find the answers. The French Protestant minister Philippe Vernier said it best:

> "Do not wait for great strength before setting out, for immobility will weaken you further. Do not wait to see very clearly before starting: one has to walk toward the light. Have you strength enough to take the first step? Courage enough to accomplish this tiny little act of fidelity or of reparation, the necessity of which is apparent to you? Take this step! Perform this act! You will be astonished to feel that the effort accomplished, instead of having exhausted your strength, has doubled it, and that you already see more clearly what you have to do next. "

Can You Analyze This Problem?

T HE ABILITY of managers to solve problems and make decisions rationally has long been assumed to be one of the valuable products of experience on the job. But close observation of their actual practices has shown that even veteran managers are likely to be very unsystematic when dealing with problems and decisions. And their hit-or-miss methods often produce decisions based on erroneous conclusions, which means that the decisions must also be wrong.

Some years ago, the surprisingly inefficient ways in which managers use information led Charles H. Kepner, a social psychologist, and Benjamin B. Tregoe, a sociologist, to develop a systematic approach to problem solving and decision making. A description of the research and training methods developed by Kepner-Tregoe and Associates of Princeton, N.J., was presented to HBR readers in an earlier issue.* And by now more than 15,000 experienced managers in major corporations have been trained in their concepts of problem analysis

---

* See "Developing Decision Makers," HBR September-October 1960, p. 115.

and decision making. These concepts are shortly to be published in book form.**

Practically every manager who has taken this training has been rather rudely shocked to discover how faulty his own reasoning methods have been in handling problems and decision. Readers are therefore invited to test their own reasoning powers against the problems presented in the case history, based directly on an actual situation, set forth below.

The Burred Panels

The problems to be solved are presented in the form of dialogues between various managers in a plant which manufactures quarter panels — the body parts that cover the front quarters of the car, including the wheels. The quarter panel is the successor to the fender, and is the part most often damaged in collisions in traffic accidents. This plant has 3,000 employees and makes not only quarter panels but many other smaller parts and components for two of the models sold by one of the Big Three auto companies.

The panels are made on four separate production lines, each line headed by a huge hydraulic press that stamps the panels out of sheet-steel blanks. When the flat steel arrives at the plant from various suppliers by rail, it is unloaded and carried to a machine which cuts identical-size blanks for all four hydraulic presses. Blanks go to the presses by forklift trucks in pallet stacks of 40 each, and the schedule is so arranged that there is always a supply on hand when the presses are started up on the morning shift.

** Charles H. Kepner and Benjamin B. Tregoe, *The Rational Manager*, edited with an introduction by Perrin Stryker (New York, McGraw-Hill Book Company, Inc.).

The Principals

Since this problem, like any other management problem, involves different types of people, the following brief descriptions of the characters, whose names have been disguised, may be useful:

- *Oscar Burger, Plant Manager — a tough manager in his late fifties; known for his willingness to listen to others; considered anti-union by the employees.*
- *Robert Polk, Production Chief — a hard-nosed driver, very able technically, but quick-tongued and inclined to favor certain subordinates; also considered anti-union by the employees.*
- *Ben Peters, Quality Control Manager — reserved, quiet, and cautious when dealing with others; extremely confident in his figures.*
- *Ralph Coggin, Industrial Relations Manager — a fairly typical personnel manager; sympathetic to employees; relies on human relations techniques in dealing with the union.*
- *Andy Patella, Shop Steward — antagonistic to management and eager to prove his power; has developed rapport with Industrial Relations Manager Coggin.*
- *George Adams, Supervisor on Line 1 — steady, solid, and well respected by his men.*
- *James Farrell, Supervisor on Line 2 — irascible, ambitious, and somewhat puritanical; very anti-union.*
- *Henry Dawson, Supervisor on Line 3 — patient, warm-hearted, and genuinely liked by his men.*
- *Otto Henschel, Supervisor on Line 4 — aloof, cool, and a bit ponderous; neither liked nor disliked by his men.*

Morning Emergency

The situation opens at 11:00 A.M. on a Wednesday in the office of Plant Manager Oscar Burger, who has called an emergency meeting.

Fifty minutes ago he learned from Production Chief Bob Polk that nearly 10 percent of the panels coming off Lines 1 and 2 were being rejected by Quality Control because of burrs and other rough spots.

BURGER: I've called you in here because we're in real trouble if we can't lick this reject problem fast. The company needs all the panels we can ship, and more, if it's going to catch up with this new model market. Both new models of the Panther and the Cheetah are going over big, and if we slow down on panels, the old man in Detroit will be on my neck fast. So let's get all the facts out on the table and run this thing down before lunch. Bob here tells me Line 1 started putting out rejects about three minutes after the end of the 10 o'clock relief break and Line 2 went wild about 9:30. Bob, suppose you tell us just what you've found out so far.

POLK: You've covered it, Oscar. Farrell, the supervisor now on Line 2, says he's checked several times to see if these burrs in the panels are being caused by something in the sheets, but he hasn't found anything suspicious. Sheets all look nice and clean going into the press, but many come out rough as hell. He says the inspectors report that rejects rose from the normal one or two an hour to eight or nine in the last hour. On Line 1, George Adams says it's about the same story, and he can't figure it out — it just started up suddenly after the relief break.

BURGER: Doesn't Farrell or Adams have *any* idea why it started?

POLK: Well, Farrell is sure it's deliberate sabotage by the draw-press operators, but he can't catch them at it. He says it's not hard to produce burrs and rough spots if a man positions a sheet just slightly wrong. He says the men on his line are mad as hell over his suspending Joe Valenti yesterday, and he had another argument when Valenti came in this morning against orders and tried to take back his press job. Farrell called the guard and had Valenti escorted to the gate.

BURGER: What's that? I never head about this. What's wrong with Valenti? (*He turns to Industrial Relations Manager Coggin.*) Ralph, what about this?

COGGIN: Oh, I don't think it's all Valenti's fault. He and Farrell have been at it for a long time, as you no doubt know, arguing over management's rights. Farrell says he saw Valenti go behind the tool crib yesterday afternoon during the relief break, and Farrell swears Valenti had a bottle with him. He caught Valenti drinking on the job last year, you remember, and says he wishes he'd fired Valenti then instead of suspending him. You know how Farrell is about liquor, especially on the job. Anyway, he accused Valenti of drinking on the job. Anyway, he accused Valenti of drinking on the job again, and after some hot words he sent Valenti home for the rest of the week. Andy Patella, the shop steward, protested Farrell's action immediately, of course.

POLK: Farrell's OK, Ralph; he's doing his job.

BURGER: Let's get back to this reject problem. What has Valenti got to do with it?

COGGIN: Well, I talked with Patella, and he reports the men on all four lines are sore as hell. They made some sharp cracks about Farrell being a union-buster yesterday after the argument and again this morning when he threw Valenti out. When the drawpress on #2 started putting out a lot of rejects on Panther panels, and Quality Control reported this to Farrell, he went over to the press operator and made some suggestions on placing the sheets, or something like that. The man just glared at him and said nothing, Patella tells me, and Farrell finally walked away. The reject rate stayed high, and during the whole 15 minutes of the relief break the men from all the lines were talking together about Valenti's case. Patella says Valenti's young brother, Pete, a spot welder who works on Line 3 under Dawson, called for a walkout , and quite a few seemed to think it was a good idea — contract or no contract. Then right after the men went back to work, Line 1 started to throw off rejects at a high rate.

BURGER: What does Adams think about this, Ralph?

COGGIN: He won't completely buy that sabotage theory of Farrell's, but he admits there doesn't seem to be any other explanation. The maintenance troubleshooters have been all over the press and can't find anything wrong. The die is OK, and the hydraulic system is OK. They made some adjustments on the iron claw that removes the piece from the press, but that's all.

BURGER (*turning to Quality Control Manager Ben Peters*): Ben, what is your idea about this?

PETERS: It's hard to say what might be causing it. We've been checking the sheets from Zenith Metals we started using this morning, and they looked perfect going through the blanker. Besides, it's only on Lines 1 and 2 that we're getting burrs, so maybe we've got trouble with those presses.

POLK: I'll check it with Engineering, but I'm willing to bet my last dollar the presses are OK.

BURGER: Yes, I think you can forget about trouble in the presses, Ben. And the blanker's never given us a hard time, ever. Still, you'd better have Engineering check that too, Bob, just in case. Meanwhile, I'd like to . . . . (*He pauses while the door opens and Burger's secretary slips in and hands Peters a note.*)

PETERS: I'll be damned! My assistant Jerry tells me that Line 4 has just begun turning out a mess of burred rejects. I wouldn't have thought that slow old line could go haywire like that — those high-speed presses on the other lines, maybe, but not on Henschel's steady old #4 rocking along at 50 panels an hour.

POLK: Well, that seems to knock out a theory I was getting ready to offer. With #4 acting up, too, it looks like the press speeds aren't to blame. Now I guess we won't have long to wait before Dawson's line also starts bugging up the blanks.

COGGIN: Maybe #3 won't go sour if what Patella says about Dawson is true. He says Dawson's men would go all out for him if he asked them, and I gather Patella hasn't had much success selling them on his anticompany tactics.

BURGER: What's he peddling now?

COGGIN: Same old stuff. He claims the company is trying to discredit the union with the men, especially now that contract negotiations are coming up next month. This year he's also tossed in the rumor that the company will threaten to abandon this plant and move out of the state if the union does not accept the local package of benefits management offers in negotiations.

BURGER: That's stupid. Hell, when will the union wake up and give us a fair days's work for the pay they're getting? But let's stop this chatter and get after these rejects. Check anything and everything you can think of. We can't afford to shut any line down with the factory as tight as it is on Panther panels. Let's meet back here at 4 o'clock this afternoon.

Informal Get-together

The meeting breaks up, and Polk goes to the shop floor to check on the presses and the blanker. Peters goes to his quality-control records to see when the reject rate last hit its current level. Industrial Relations Manager Coggin seeks out Patella to check on Farrell's handling of Valenti and the other men on his line. During the lunch hour in the cafeteria, an informal meeting of the four supervisors and Production Chief Bob Polk takes place.

FARRELL: I suppose you got the boss all straightened out on those rejects, Bob. That Valenti has a lot of buddies, and we'll need to keep our eyes peeled to actually catch them fouling up the stampings.

HENSCHEL: You can say that again! I've got a couple of Valenti's old buddies on my line, and ever since the burrs started showing up about 11:20, they've been extra careful. I've traced at least three rejects that I think I can attribute to him.

POLK: Keep a count on who makes the most rejects, and maybe we can pin this down to a few soreheads.

ADAMS: You fellas sound like you're on a manhunt. As for me, I think Engineering will come up with the answer. The press on my line has been making more noise than usual today, and I think there's something fishy there. Right now, Bob, I'd like your help in getting the night shift to cut down on the number of stacks of blanks they leave us for the morning runs. It'd help a lot if they'd keep it down to two stacks of 40 each. Again this morning I had four stacks cluttering up my area.

POLK: I'll see what I can do with Scheduling.

HENSCHEL: I'm with you there, Adams. I've been loaded with four stacks for the last five days running. With my slow-speed old equipment, I could manage nicely with only one stack to start off. I noticed Farrell had two stacks and Dawson had only one to start his line today, and why should they be getting favors?

DAWSON: Now, Otto, you're just jealous of my new high-speed press. You got an old clunker, and you know it. What you need is to get off that diet of Panther panels and join me banging out those shallow-draw panels for the Cheetah. Also, it might help you to smile now and then when one of your men cracks a joke. Remember that old proverb, "He that despiseth small things shall fall by little and little."

FARRELL: I can think of another proverb that you might consider, Dawson. "Spare the rod and spoil the child." Is it true that your crew is going to win a trip to Bermuda if they're all good boys and make nothing but good panels?

ADAMS: Aw, cut it, Farrell. We can't all be tough guys.

FARRELL: Well, anyway, I'm glad Dawson didn't have to cope with Valenti today. That boozer is finally out of my hair. I can't forget last year when he helped Patella spread the word that if the men would burr a lot of the stamping, they could pressure management into a better contract. I wouldn't be surprised if Valenti and Patella were in cahoots now, trying the same angle before negotiations start.

ADAMS: Relax, Farrell. You can't prove that's so. The men aren't as dumb as all that, as last year proved when they refused to believe Patella. What bugs me is those rejects this morning. Never saw so many bad burrs show up so fast.

HENSCHEL: They sure surprised me, too, but you know I think Quality Control may be a little bit overexcited about the burrs. I figure all of them could be reamed and filed out with little handwork. Put two extra men on the line, and it would be all taken care of.

FARRELL: Maybe so, but you know how Burger would feel about the extra costs on top of the lower output. And don't forget, Henschel, our high-speed presses are banging out 30 more an hour than yours. Well, I gotta get back and see what's with Valenti's buddies on my line.

Aside Conversation

All the supervisors get up and leave together. They pay no attention to Industrial Relations Manager Coggin talking with Shop Steward Patella in a corner of the cafeteria.

COGGIN: What I want to know, Patella, is why did Valenti try to get back on the line this morning against Farrell's orders?

PATELLA: Why not? Farrell was miles off base sending Joe home yesterday without telling me or you or anyone else. I was glad Joe came back and faced that s.o.b. Farrell's been getting jumpier and jumpier lately, and do you know what they say? They say he's cracking up over that poor kid of his — the little teenager who's turned out to be such a tramp. I feel sorry for him, but that's no reason why he has to take his feelings out on his men. His crew won't take it much longer, and the other crews are sore, too. You know Valenti's brother this morning over on Line 3 began talking about a walkout?

COGGIN: Yes, I heard he did. So why didn't they go out?

PATELLA: Oh, that crew of Dawson's is too company-minded, and there are some older men there who almost worship Dawson. But they'll go out if management doesn't wise up and respect their rights.

COGGIN: What about that man who got hurt last night on overtime while unloading those sheets?

PATELLA: He's been on the job for a couple of months, but he tells me he wasn't familiar with the method of blocking that Zenith Metal's uses. He's not hurt bad, but he'll get workmen's compensation OK.

COGGIN: Sure. Now how certain are you about Farrell not finding any bottle behind the tool crib after he suspended

Valenti? And are you sure you're right that there were no witnesses? You know you've got to be positive of your evidence.

PATELLA: OK, Ralph. I'm certain, I'm sure, I'm positive!

Afternoon Meeting

Three hours later, Plant Manger Burger is again in a meeting wit Production Chief Polk, Quality Control Manager Peters, and Industrial Relations Manager Coggin.

BURGER: Let's hear from you first, Bob, about that check on the presses and the blanker. Any clues to those burrs?

POLK: Nope. Everything is OK with the machinery, according to Engineering. They even thought I was nuts to be questioning them and making them double-check.

BURGER: I can imagine. But we can't overlook anything, no matter how impossible Engineering may think it is. By the way, Ben, are the rejects still running as high this afternoon?

PETERS: Higher. Line 1 is lousing up nine or ten an hour, Line 2 is ruining about a dozen, and Line 4 is burring about seven an hour.

BURGER: What about Line 3?

PETERS: Nothing so far. Dawson's line has been clean as a whistle. But, with Valenti's brother on the line, we can expect trouble any time.

POLK: Maybe not. Dawson's reject rates have always been a bit lower than the others'.

BURGER: That so? How do you account for that?

COGGIN: How about better supervision accounting for it? Dawson's men always seem to take more pride in their work that the other men do, and they really operate as a team. The other day I heard two of his men talking about one of their crew who apparently was getting careless, and they decided to straighten him out themselves, without bothering Dawson. When you get that kind of voluntary discipline, you've got real supervision.

BURGER: Glad to hear that some of our men feel responsible for doing good work.

POLK: Dawson's crew is OK. One of his men will always tip me off early if they're getting low on blanks, but the night shift on that line is mighty careless. That crew left Dawson's line with only a half-hour's stack of blanks to start up with this morning.

PETERS: By the way, Bob, have you heard that some of the men on the other crews are calling his men "Dawson's Darlings"? The rumor is that those shallow Cheetah panels are easier to make, and someone played favorites when they gave that production run to Dawson's crew.

POLK: That's crazy. We gave those panels to Dawson's line because this makes it easier for the Shipping Department, and they just aren't any easier to make — you know that.

PETERS: I know, but that's what the men say, and I thought you'd like to be cut in on the grapevine.

COGGIN: If the men think the deep panels are a harder job, maybe there's something to it. I've heard this story, too, and there's a chance the union may try to review our rates and standards one of these days.

POLK: Yeah? Well, I say nuts to it. If those items go on the agenda, then Patella might as well be running this shop. Why don't we ask the union: "How about making up for that half-hour Line 2 lost this morning while Valenti argued with Farrell about his suspension?"

COGGIN: While you're asking, ask Farrell why he didn't call me before suspending Valenti yesterday. What a mess Farrell put us in!

BURGER: What do you mean, Ralph?

COGGIN: Just that we've got a real big grievance coming up, for sure. Patella tells me that after Farrell suspended Valenti yesterday, he went looking behind the tool crib and couldn't find any sign of a liquor bottle. Also, Patella claims there were no witnesses around when Farrell accused Valenti of drinking on the job. It's going to be impossible for Farrell to prove he wasn't acting merely on his suspicions, without evidence. And the union is sure to hit us hard with this, especially with contract negotiations coming up.

BURGER: Damn it, Farrell should have known better! This isn't the first time he's been tough with a man, but he's got to learn to use better judgment. Bob, you'd better have a talk with him right away. See if anything special is chewing him. Maybe a little firm advice from you will sharpen him up.

POLK: OK, Oscar, but Farrell's a very good man, and we ought to back him up on this completely.

COGGIN: If you do, you're going to have real trouble with the union. Patella says if we don't drop the charge against Valenti and reinstate him, he's going to propose a strike vote, and he claims the men will positively go out. It looks like they have a clear case against Farrell and, except for Dawson's men, a lot of them seem plenty sore. And those rejects they're producing are telling you so, loud and clear.

POLK: Oscar, we can't undercut Farrell! If we do, we're playing right into the union's hands. It's obvious that Valenti is in collusion with Patella on this, and they're framing Farrell to get themselves a hot issue for the contract negotiations. I say we should charge the union with framing Farrell and willfully producing rejects. If they try to strike, get an injunction immediately so we can keep production up and satisfy Detroit.

BURGER: Not so fast, Bob. I'd rather first try to get the union off our backs before they seriously start talking about a strike. Ralph, what about that demand the local union agent told you he was going to make — something like 10 minutes' extra wash-up time? If we gave in to him on this, do you think he could hold Patella in line on this Farrell-Valenti problem?

COGGIN: Probably. But you would want to find some way for Patella to save face, as well as Farrell.

BURGER: You may be right, but we can't let Patella think he can go on using this sabotage technique of his. I want to mull this over some more before deciding what our answer will have to be. Meanwhile, Ben, you keep a close check on the reject rates. And you, Bob, check on the operation on Line 3 to see if there really is anything to that rumor about our favoring Dawson's crew. Ralph, see what you can find out about that extra wash-up time deal and how Patella feels about it. That's about all I can suggest for now. Let's meet again tomorrow at 10 o'clock and wind this thing up.

Burger's Dilemma

The meeting breaks up and the managers go back to their respective jobs. Plant Manager Burger spends some time by himself trying to resolve the dilemma. He sees two choices facing him: (1) back up Farrell and risk a strike that might be stopped by injunction, or (2) avoid a strike by undercutting Farrell, reinstating Valenti, and asking the men to cooperate in eliminating excess rejects. He does not like either of the alternatives, and hopes he can think of some better way to get out of this jam. At least, he tells himself, he has a night to sleep on it.

Your Analysis?

Has Plant Manager Burger analyzed the situation correctly? You are invited to think through this situation for yourself and decide how you would go about solving it. You will be able to compare your results with the solutions that will be presented in Part II in the July-August issue of HBR, which will describe the Kepner-Tregoe concepts and procedures for problem analysis.

Analyzing That Problem

I N THIS EXAMPLE, there are two issues, the burred panels and the conflict between workers and supervisors. However, the crux of the matter is to determine the cause of the bad panels because that will determine the corrective action to be taken on both problems.

The first step in analyzing the problem is to recognize that everyone is reacting to symptoms and emotions. No one knows what is causing the problems. The second step is to identify the possible causes of the burred panels, which from the information supplied in the problem are: (1) sabotage, (2) equipment problems, and (3) the new blanks from Zenith.

The next step is to analyze available information to see if the facts support any of these theories. There should be a correlation between when and where burrs are occurring and either personnel problems, equipment problems, or the new material. Going through the case, we can find the following facts (in sequence):

1. Blanks come in on pallets of 40 each.
2. Line 1 started having problems 3 minutes after the 10:00 break (which is later specified as 15 minutes).

3. Line 2 started having problems at 9:30.

4. Use of the new Zenith panels started in the morning. Later in the case, it is mentioned that the new Zenith panels were unloaded after the regular night shift ended.

5. Line 4 produces at the rate of 50 panels/hour and started having problems at 11:20.

6. Lines 1 and 4 started production with four stacks of panels, Line 2 with two, and Line 3 with one.

7. Line 3 is producing shallow-draw Cheetah panels; the other lines are producing deep-draw Panther panels.

8. Lines 1,2, and 3 produce at 30 panels/hour above Line 4, or 80/hour.

9. Line 1 has a reject rate of 9/hour; Line 2 of 12/hour; Line 4 of 7/hour. The normal reject rate is 1 to 2/hour.

10. Line 2 started 1/2 hour late because of an argument.

There is no evidence that equipment is the problem. Besides being checked, it is highly unlikely three presses of two different types would all start acting up on the same day. Clearly, this was an unusual circumstance where the production system was operating far outside of its normal limits in three machines out of four. While Line 3 has no rejects, it also has the distinction of producing shallow-draw panels. So, we might suspect that this explains the lack of burrs, not the equipment.

There is good reason to suspect the rejects were caused by sabotage. All of the men were angry at Valenti's suspension and the problem started on Farrell's line. It would also be logical for the problem to spread to the other lines, starting at different times.

However, there is no hard evidence that sabotage is the problem — no one has been caught doing anything wrong.

There is also the question of why Line 3 has experienced no problems. It could be because Dawson is liked, but with Valenti's brother on the line, there is also reason to expect Line 3 to have more personnel problems. Another possible explanation for there being no rejects on Line 3 is that it is producing shallow-draw panels.

Emotionally, sabotage looks like a pretty sure thing, but there are no facts to support that conclusion other than that most of the men were upset at the suspension of Valenti. We have a correlation between angry employees and a sudden increase in rejects, but two events happening at the same time is not sufficient to establish a cause-and-effect relationship. This is probably the most common cause of mis-diagnosing problems.

Digging further into the data, we can see if there is any correlation between when the rejects started and when they would have started if the new Zenith blanks were the problem. Since the Zenith blanks were not unloaded until after the end of the night shift, it can be assumed that the stacks left for each press by the night shift were all of the old material. Taking into account the 15-minute break time, the half-hour delayed start on Line 2, the production rate of each press, and the beginning stacks for each machine, we can calculate when rejects could have been expected to occur if the new material was the problem. As you can see by Table A-1, there is almost perfect correlation between the expected and actual times. Line 3 did not have any rejects, which can be attributed to the difference in draw depth. We can therefore safely conclude that the source of the problem is the Zenith blanks which must somehow be different from the previous material.

In practice, the next step would be to run a controlled test using the old material if any was available. If not, the supervisors could run one of the lines to see if the reject rate dropped

Table A.1 Correlation Between Expected and Actual Times

LINE	DRAW TYPE	NO. OF BLANKS	PROD. RATE	CALCULATED TIME FOR REJECTS TO START	ACTUAL TIME REJECTS STARTED
1	Deep	160	80/hr	10:15	10:18
2	Deep	80	80/hr	9:30	9:30
3	Shallow	40	80/hr	8:30	—
4	Deep	160	50/hr	11:27	11:20

back to its normal range. Another option would be to switch the men from Line 3 with one of the other lines to see if the problems followed the men or the production line.

This analysis is abbreviated to some extent. For a more detailed discussion, see "How To Analyze That Problem" by Perrin Stryker. It is available as Reprint No. 65412 from: HBS Publishing Division, Operations, Boston, Massachusetts 02163-0014, (617) 495-6117.

References and Suggested Reading

1. Ackoff, Russell L. *The Art of Problem Solving.* (New York: John Wiley & Sons, 1978).
2. Amsden, Robert T.; Butler, Howard E.; and Amsden, Davida A. *SPC Simplified.* (White Plains, NY: Quality Resources, 1986).
3. Bacon, Kenneth H. "Connecticut Grades Its Schools and Holds Officials Responsible." *The Wall Street Journal,* (April 4, 1990), A1, A6.
4. Berry, Leonard L.; Parasuraman, A.; and Zeithaml, Valarie A. "The Service-Quality Puzzle." *Business Horizons,* (September- October 1988), 35-43.
5. "Being the Boss." *Inc.,* (October 1989), 49-65.
6. Blanchard, Kenneth and Johnson, Spencer. *The One-Minute Manager.* (New York: Berkley Books, 1983).
7. Bodenstab, Charles J. "Keeping Tabs On Your Company." *Inc.,* (August 1989), 131-132.
8. Brokaw, Leslie and Lammers, Teri. "What Motivates Managers." *Inc.,* (June 1989), 115.
9. Burt, David N. "Managing Suppliers Up to Speed." *Harvard Business Review,* (July-August 1989), 127-135.
10. Camp, Robert C. *Benchmarking.* (Milwaukee: ASQC Quality Press, 1989).
11. Caulkins, Laurel. "The America That Works." *Business Month,* (July 1990), 5.
12. Charlier, Marj. "At an Arizona Mine Workers Were Wooed Away From the Union." *The Wall Street Journal,* (August 8, 1989), A1, A6.
13. Cooper, Ken. *Conflict Management.* Audiotape. (Fullerton, CA: TDM/McGraw-Hill).

14. Crosby, Philip B. *Quality Is Free*. (New York: New American Library, 1979).
15. Cusumano, Michael A. "Manufacturing Innovation: Lessons from the Japanese Auto Industry." *Sloan Management Review*, (Fall 1988), 29-39.
16. Deming, W. Edwards. *Quality, Productivity, and Competitive Position*. (Boston: MIT Center for Advanced Engineering Study, 1982).
17. Dickinson, Daniel. *It's Their Business Too*. (New York: American Management Association, 1985).
18. Drucker, Peter F. "How To Measure White-collar Productivity." *The Wall Street Journal*, (November 26, 1985), A10.
19. Garvin, David A. "Competing on the Eight dimensions of Quality." *Harvard Business Review*, (November-December 1987), 101-109.
20. Harper, Steven C. "Now That the Dust Has Settled; Learning From Japanese Management." *Business Horizons*, (July-August 1988), 43-51.
21. Hayes, Robert H. "Why Japanese Factories Work." *Harvard Business Review*, (July-August 1981), 57-66.
22. Hayes, Robert H. *Reflections On Japanese Factory Management*, Boston: HBS Case Services, reprint #9-681-084 (Rev. 4/83).
23. Hayes, Robert H. and Clark, Kim B. "Why Some Factories Are More Productive than Others." *Harvard Business Review*, (September-October 1986), 66-73.
24. Hefley, James. "Sales Representatives Need Support From Their Supervisors." *Management Review*, (February 1988), 9-10.
25. Hoerr, John. "The Cultural Revolution at A. O. Smith." *Business Week*, (May 29, 1989), 66-67.
26. Imai, Masaaki. *Kaizen*. (New York: Random House Business Division, 1986).
27. Ishikawa, Kaoru. *What Is Total Quality Control?* (Englewood Cliffs, NJ: Prentice Hall, 1987).
28. Janson, Robert L. "Graphic Indicators of Operations." *Harvard Business Review*, (November-December 1980), 164-170.
29. Judson, Arnold S. "The Awkward Truth about Productivity." *Harvard Business Review*, (September-October 1982), 93-97.
30. Kanter, Rosabeth M. "Follow Up and Follow Through." *Harvard Business Review*, (March-April 1990), 8.
31. Kaufman, Steve. "Quest For Quality." *Business Month*, (May 1989), 61-65.
32. Kaydos, W. J. "Manufacturing Market Share." *Business Horizons*, (May-June 1984), 37-39.

33. Kehrer, Daniel M. "The Miracle of Theory Q." *Business Month,* (September 1989), 45-49.

34. Kelly, Kevin. "That Old Time Accounting Isn't Good Enough Any More." *Business Week,* (June 6, 1988), 112.

35. Kepner, Charles H. and Tregoe, Benjamin B. *The New Rational Manager.* (Princeton, NJ: Princeton Research Press, 1981).

36. Klein, Janice A. "Why Supervisors Resent Employee Involvement." *Harvard Business Review,* (September-October 1984), 87-95.

37. Kovach, Kenneth A. "What Motivates Employees? Workers and Supervisors Give Different Answers." *Business Horizons,* (September-October 1987), 58-65.

38. "Labor Letter." *The Wall Street Journal,* (February 11, 1987), A1.

39. "Labor Letter." *The Wall Street Journal,* (January 16, 1990), A1.

40. "Labor Letter." *The Wall Street Journal,* (May 5, 1990), A1.

41. Lawler, Edward E. and Mohrman, Susan A. "Quality Circles After the Fad." *Harvard Business Review,* (January-February 1985), 65-71.

42. Likert, Rensis. "Measuring Organizational Performance." *Harvard Business Review,* (March-April 1958), 41-50.

43. Mariotti, John L. "How A U.S. Manufacturer Is Beating Very Tough Foreign Competition." *Boardroom Reports,* (March 1, 1988), 3-4.

44. McNamara, Carlton P. "Productivity is Management's Problem." *Business Horizons,* (March-April 1983), 55-61.

45. *Measuring productivity of insurance offices yields major savings* — Case Study 23. (Houston: American Productivity Center, 1983).

46. Myers, Scott M. "Who Are Your Motivated Workers?" *How Successful Executives Handle People.* (Boston: Harvard Business Review Publishing Division), 31-46.

47. Moriarty, Rowland T. and Swartz, Gordon S. "Automation to Boost Sales and Marketing." *Harvard Business Review,* (January-February 1989), 100-108.

48. Naylor, Thomas H. "U.S., Soviet Employees Share Common Alienation." *The Charlotte Observer,* (July 9, 1989), 1D,4D.

49. Nelson-Horchler, Joani. "The Pay Revolt Brews." *Business Week,* (June 18, 1990), 22-36.

50. Nolan, Thomas W. and Provost, Lloyd P. "Understanding Variation." *Quality Progress,* (May 1990), 70-78.

51. O'Boyle, Thomas F. "GE Refrigerator Woes Illustrate the Hazards In Changing a Product." *The Wall Street Journal,* (May 7, 1990), A1, A5.

52. Parkinson, C. Northcote. *Parkinson's Law.* (Boston: Houghton-Mifflin, 1957).

53. Patton, John A. "Assembly-line Accountability Off the Factory Floor." *The Wall Street Journal*, (August 1, 1986), A12.
54. Pennar, Karen. "The Productivity Paradox." *Business Week*, (June 6, 1988), 100-102.
55. Peters, Thomas J. and Waterman, Robert H. *In Search of Excellence*. (New York: Harper & Row, 1982).
56. "The Piecework Price." *Inc.*, (January 1988), 84.
57. Port, Otis; King, Resa; and Hampton, William J. "How the New Math of Productivity Adds Up." *Business Week*, (June 6, 1988), 103-113.
58. Rickards, Tudor. *Problem Solving Through Creative Analysis*. (Epping, Essex, England: Gower Press Limited, 1974).
59. Roman, Mark B. "Lean and Mean, Inc." *Success*, (December 1988), 40-41.
60. Runcie, John F. "By Days I Make the Cars." *Harvard Business Review*, (May- June 1980), 106-115.
61. Shay, David, "Peat Marwick's Secrets of Increased White-collar Productivity." *Boardroom Reports*, (August 15, 1988), 15.
62. Shingo, Shigeo, *Zero Quality Control: Source Inspection and the Poka-yoke System*. (Cambridge, Mass.: Productivity Press, Inc., 1986).
63. Sirota, David. "Productivity Management." *Harvard Business Review*, (September-October 1966), 111-116.
64. Skinner, Wickham. "The Productivity Paradox." *Harvard Business Review*, (July-August 1986), 55-59.
65. Stack, Bill. "IJ's Laptop Solution." *The Foodservice Distributor*, (March 1989), 38-44.
66. Stryker, Perrin. "Can You Analyze This Problem?" *Harvard Business Review*, (May-June 1965), 73-78.
67. Stryker, Perrin. "How To Analyze That Problem." *Harvard Business Review*, (July-August 1965), 99-110.
68. Thompson, Donald B. "Back To Basics." *Industry Week*, (December 10, 1984), 73-75.
69. Waterman, Robert H., Jr. *The Renewal Factor*. (New York: Bantam Books, 1987).
70. Weiss, Andrew. "Simple Truths of Japanese Manufacturing." *Harvard Business Review*, (July-August 1984), 119-125.
71. Werther, William B., Jr. "Out of the Productivity Box." *Business Horizons*, (September-October 1982), 51-59.
72. Wheelright, Steven C. "Japan: Where Operations Are Really Strategic." *Harvard Business Review*, (July-August 1981), 67-74.

73. White, Joseph B. and Guiles, Melinda Grenier, "GM's Plan for Saturn, To Beat Small Imports, Trails Original Goals." *The Wall Street Journal*, (July 9, 1990), A1, A4

74. Wiggenhorn, William. "Motorola U: When Training Becomes an Education." *Harvard Business Review*, (July-August 1990), 71-83.

75. Zellner, Wendy. "For Auto Workers, It's Team Spirit vs. Suspicion." *Business Week*, (July 10, 1989), 61.

76. Zemke, Ron and Bell, Chip R. *Service Wisdom*. (Minneapolis, MN: Lakewood Books, 1989).

Endnotes

1. Masaaki Imai, *Kaizen*, (New York: Random House Business Division, 1986), 1-2.
2. A good discussion of management's role in improving productivity is given by: Carlton P. McNamara, "Productivity Is Management's Problem," *Business Horizons*, (March-April 1983), 55-61.
3. Steve Kaufman, "Quest For Quality," *Business Month*, (May 1989), 61.
4. Janice A. Klein, "Why Supervisors Resent Employee Involvement," *Harvard Business Review*, (September-October 1984), 87-95.
5. W. J. Kaydos, "Manufacturing Market Share," *Business Horizons*, (May-June 1984), 37-39.
6. Karen Pennar, "The Productivity Paradox," *Business Week*, (June 6, 1988), 100-102.
7. Otis Port, "How the New Math of Productivity Adds Up," *Business Week*, (June 6, 1988), 112.
8. David A. Garvin, "Competing on the Eight Dimensions of Quality," *Harvard Business Review*, (November-December 1987), 101-109.
9. Leonard L. Berry, A. Parasuraman, and Valarie A. Zeithaml, "The Service-Quality Puzzle," *Business Horizons*, (September-October 1988), 37.
10. Robert H. Hayes, "Why Japanese Factories Work," *Harvard Business Review*, (July-August 1981), 61.
11. Robert H. Hayes, "Reflections on Japanese Management," Harvard Business School Case Services, Reprint #9-681-004:17.
12. "Labor Letter," *The Wall Street Journal*, (May 5, 1990), A1.

13. Thomas J. Peters and Robert H. Waterman, *In Search of Excellence*, (New York: Harper & Row, 1982).

14. Leslie Brokaw and Teri Lammers, "What Motivates Managers," *Inc.*, (June 1989), 115.

15. Robert H. Waterman, Jr., *The Renewal Factor*, (New York: Bantam Books, 1987), pp. 255-256. This describes how Humana improved performance in their hospitals by using performance measures. Also how a bank lost customers by not measuring and rewarding desired behavior.

16. Thomas H. Naylor, "U.S., Soviet Employees Share Common Alienation," *The Charlotte Observer*, (July 9, 1989), 4D.

17. Kenneth A. Kovach, "What Motivates Employees: Workers and Supervisors Give Different Answers," *Business Horizons*, (September-October 1987), 61.

18. Peters and Waterman, *In Search of Excellence*, 121-125.

19. Kovach, "What Motivates Workers...", 61.

20. Kaufman, "Quest For Quality," 61.

21. Brokaw and Lammers, "What Motivates Managers," 115.

22. Scott M. Meyers, "Who Are Your Motivated Workers?" *How Successful Executives Handle People*, (Boston: Harvard Business School Publishing Division), 31-46.

23. Michael A. Cusumano, "Manufacturing Innovation: Lessons from the Japanese Auto Industry," *Sloan Management Review*, (Fall 1988), 34.

24. Bill Stack, "IJ's Laptop Solution," *The Foodservice Distributor*, (March 1989).

25. Kaydos, "Manufacturing Market Share," 38.

26. Steven C. Wheelright, "Japan: Where Operations Really Are Strategic," *Harvard Business Review*, (July-August 1981), 67-74.

27. Mark B. Roman, "Lean and Mean, Inc." *Success* (December 1988), 40.

28. Roman, "Lean and Mean, Inc.", 41.

29. Rensis Likert, "Measuring Organizational Performance," *Harvard Business Review*, (March-April 1958), 41-50.

30. Donald B. Thompson, "Back To Basics," *Industry Week*, (December 10, 1984), 75.

31. Charles J. Bodenstab, "Keeping Tabs On Your Company," *Inc.*, (August 1989), 131-132.

32. Kevin Kelly, "That Old Time Accounting Isn't Good Enough Any More," *Business Week*, (June 6, 1988), 112.

33. Wickham Skinner, "The Productivity Paradox," *Harvard Business Review*, 57.

34. Deming, 48.

35. Kaoru Ishikawa, *What Is Quality Control?* (Englewood Cliffs: Prentice-Hall, 1987), 198.

36. Charles M. Kepner and Benjamin B. Tregoe, *The New Rational Manager*, (Princeton: Princeton Research Press, 1981). This is an excellent reference on diagnosing problems.

37. Shigeo Shingo, *Zero Quality Control: Source Inspection and the Poka-yoke System*, (Cambridge, Mass.: Productivity Press, 1986), xvi.

38. Tudor Rickards, *Problem Solving Through Creative Analysis*, (Epping, Essex, England: Gower Press Limited, 1974). A useful reference for brainstorming and other problem-solving methods.

39. Russell L. Ackoff, *The Art of Problem Solving*, (New York: John Wiley & Sons), 1978, 50-53.

40. Cusumano, "Manufacturing Innovation: Lessons from the Japanese Auto Industry," 48.

41. Robert C. Camp, *Benchmarking*, (Milwaukee: ASQC Quality Press, 1989), xii.

42. Imai, *Kaizen*, 47.

43. C. Northcote Parkinson, *Parkinson's Law* (Boston: Houghton-Mifflin, 1957).

44. James Hefley, "Sales Representatives Need Support From Their Supervisors," *Management Review*, (February, 1988), 9.

45. John F. Runcie, "By Days I Make the Cars" *Harvard Business Review*, (May-June 1980), 111.

46. Personal commentary by Tom Gelb, VP-Continuous Improvement for Harley-Davidson.

47. Imai, *Kaizen*, 16-21.

48. "Labor Letter," *The Wall Street Journal*, (February 11, 1987), A1.

49. "Labor Letter," *The Wall Street Journal*, (January 16, 1990), A1.

50. Daniel Dickinson, *It's Their Business, Too: A Manager's Guide to Employee Awareness*, (New York: American Management Association, 1985). This is an excellent summary of how employees feel about business in general and relations within their company. Although some of the survey data is now several years old, more recent information indicates there has been no substantial change in attitudes.

51. "Being the Boss" *Inc.*, (October 1989), 50.

52. Personal note from John Mariotti, President, Huffy Bicycles, Inc.

53. Hayes, "Why Japanese Factories Work," 64.

54. Steven C. Harper, ""Now That the Dust Has Settled: Learning From Japanese Management," *Business Horizons*, (July-August 1988), 48.

55. Thomas F. O'Boyle, "GE Refrigerator Woes Illustrate the Hazards In Changing a Product," *The Wall Street Journal*, (May 5, 1990), A1.
56. Kovach, "What Motivates Employees?...", 59.
57. Wendy Zellner, "For Auto Workers, Its Team Spirit vs. Suspicion," *Business Week*, (July 10, 1989), 61.
58. David Sirota, "Productivity Management," *Harvard Business Review*, (September-October 1966), 111-116.
59. Deming, 40-42.
60. "The Piecework Price," *Inc.*, (January 1988), 84.
61. Skinner, "The Productivity Paradox," 57.
62. Sirota, "Productivity Management," 111.
63. Marj Charlier, "At an Arizona Mine, Workers Were Wooed Away From the Union." *The Wall Street Journal*, (August 8, 1989), A6.
64. John Hoerr, "The Cultural Revolution at A.O. Smith," *Business Week*, (May 29, 1989), 66.
65. Personal note from Tom Gelb, VP-Continuous Improvement for Harley-Davidson.
66. Joani Nelson-Horchler, "The Pay Revolt Brews," *Business Week*, (June 18, 1990), 33.
67. Nelson-Horchler, 34.
68. Rosabeth M. Kanter, "Follow-up and Follow-through," *Harvard Business Review*, (March-April 1990), 8.
69. Joseph B. White and Melinda Grenier Guiles, "GM's Plan for Saturn, To Beat Small Imports, Trails Original Goals," *The Wall Street Journal*, (July 9, 1990), A1, A4.
70. Harper, "Now That the Dust Has Settled: Learning from Japanese Management," 47.
71. Laurel Caulkins, "The America That Works," *Business Month*, (July 1990), 5.
72. John L. Mariotti, "How A U.S. Manufacturer Is Beating Very Tough Foreign Competition," *Boardroom Reports*, (March 1, 1988) 3.
73. Edward E. Lawler and Susan A. Mohrman, "Quality Circles After the Fad," *Harvard Business Review*, (January-February 1985), 65-71.
74. Ken Cooper, *Conflict Management*, audiotape, TDM/McGraw-Hill.
75. Daniel M. Kehrer, "The Miracle of Theory Q," *Business Month*, (September 1989), 48.
76. David N. Burt, "Managing Suppliers Up to Speed," *Harvard Business Review*, (July-August 1989), 129.
77. Burt, 133.

78. Thomas W. Nolan and Lloyd P. Provost, "Understanding Variation," *Quality Progress*, (May 1990), 70-78. This is a very readable and informative discussion of variation.

79. Robert H. Hayes and Kim B. Clark, "Why Some Factories Are More Productive than Others," *Harvard Business Review*, (September-October 1986), 67.

80. Arnold S. Judson, "The Awkward Truth about Productivity," *Harvard Business Review*, (September-October 1982), 93-97, is a good discussion of management's role in improving productivity and why productivity improvement programs fail. Carlton P. McNamara, "Productivity Is Management's Problem," is another good article on the subject.

81. Hayes and Clark, p. 67, cites an actual case where this was true, but just about any company can provide numerous similar examples.

82. David Shay, "Peat Marwick's Secrets of Increased White-collar Productivity," *Boardroom Reports*, (August 15, 1988), 15.

83. John A. Patton, "Assembly-line Accountability Off the Factory Floor," *The Wall Street Journal*, (August 1, 1986), A12.

84. Peter F. Drucker, "How to Measure White-collar Productivity," *The Wall Street Journal*, (November 26, 1985), A10.

85. *Measuring Productivity of Insurance Offices Yields Major Savings* (Houston: American Productivity Center, 1983), Case Study #23.

86. Rowland T. Moriarty and Gordon S. Swartz, "Automation to Boost Sales and Marketing," *Harvard Business Review*, (January-February 1989), 100.

87. Ron Zemke and Chip R. Bell, *Service Wisdom*, (Minneapolis: Lakewood Publications, 1989), 85.

88. Kenneth H. Bacon, "Connecticut Grades Its Schools and Holds Officials Responsible," *The Wall Street Journal*, (April 4, 1990), A1.

89. Bacon, A1.

90. William Wiggenhorn, "Motorola U: When Training Becomes an Education, *Harvard Business Review*, (July-August 1990), 71-83. A very good discussion which illustrates that getting positive results from training is not all that easy.

About the Author

WILL KAYDOS is a recognized consultant, author, and speaker in quality and productivity improvement. His technical knowledge and extensive practical experience provide a unique perspective on how to achieve a high level of performance in any business activity using techniques consistent with the "Total Quality" philosophy.

Mr. Kaydos has more than twenty-five years of experience as a manager and consultant in manufacturing and administrative positions in a wide variety of industries. Prior to founding The Decision Group in Charlotte, North Carolina, he was the senior manufacturing and financial officer for a $160 million company. He is the author of *Exceeding Expectations*, publisher of the management advisory letter "The Decision Maker," and the author of numerous articles. He is a Certified Management Consultant and holds a B.S. degree from Clarkson University and an M.B.A. in Operations Management from the Wharton School.

Index

Books from Productivity Press

Productivity Press publishes books that empower individuals and companies to achieve excellence in quality, productivity, and the creative involvement of all employees. Through steadfast efforts to support the vision and strategy of continuous improvement, Productivity Press delivers today's leading-edge tools and techniques gathered directly from industry leaders around the world. Call toll-free (800) 394-6868 for our free catalog.

Handbook for Productivity Measurement and Improvement

William F. Christopher and Carl G. Thor, eds.

An unparalleled resource! In over 100 chapters, nearly 80 front-runners in the quality movement reveal the evolving theory and specific practices of world-class organizations. Spanning a wide variety of industries and business sectors, they discuss quality and productivity in manufacturing, service industries, profit centers, administration, nonprofit and government institutions, health care and education. Contributors include Robert C. Camp, Peter F. Drucker, Jay W. Forrester, Joseph M. Juran, Robert S. Kaplan, John W. Kendrick, Yasuhiro Monden, and Lester C. Thurow. Comprehensive in scope and organized for easy reference, this compendium belongs in every company and academic institution concerned with business and industrial viability.
ISBN 1-56327-007-2 / 1344 pages / $90.00 / Order HPM-B144

Corporate Diagnosis
Meeting Global Standards for Excellence

Thomas L. Jackson with Constance E. Dyer

All too often, strategic planning neglects an essential first step -and final step- diagnosis of the organization's current state. What's required is a systematic review of the critical factors in organizational learning and growth, factors that require monitoring, measurement, and management to ensure that your company competes successfully. This executive workbook provides a step-by-step method for diagnosing an organization's strategic health and measuring its overall competitiveness against world class standards. With checklists, charts, and detailed explanations, *Corporate Diagnosis* is a practical instruction manual. The pillars of Jackson's diagnostic system are strategy, structure, and capability. Detailed diagnostic questions in each area are provided as guidelines for developing your own self-assessment survey.
ISBN 1-56327-086-2 / 115 pages / $65.00 / Order CDIAG-B144

PRODUCTIVITY PRESS, DEPT. BK, P.O. BOX 13390, PORTLAND, OR 97213-0390
Telephone: 1-800-394-6868   Fax: 1-800-394-6286

Implementing a Lean Management System
Thomas L. Jackson with Karen R. Jones

Does your company think and act ahead of technological change, ahead of the customer, and ahead of the competition? Thinking strategically requires a company to face these questions with a clear future image of itself. *Implementing a Lean Management System* lays out a comprehensive management system for aligning the firm's vision of the future with market realities. Based on Hoshin management, the Japanese strategic planning method used by top managers for driving TQM throughout an organization, Lean Management is about deploying vision, strategy, and policy to all levels of daily activity. It is an eminently practical methodology emerging out of the implementation of continuous improvement methods and employee involvement. The key tools of this book builds on the knowledge of the worker, multi-skilling, and an understanding of the role and responsibilities of the new lean manufacturer.
ISBN 1-56327-085-4 / 150 pages / $65.00 / Order ILMS-B144

Learning Organizations
Developing Cultures for Tomorrow's Workplace
Sarita Chawla and John Renesch, Editors

The ability to learn faster than your competition may be the only sustainable competitive advantage! A learning organization is one where people continually expand their capacity to create results they truly desire, where new and expansive patterns of thinking are nurtured, where collective aspiration is set free, and where people are continually learning how to learn together. This compilation of 34 powerful essays, written by recognized experts worldwide, is rich in concept and theory as well as application and example. An inspiring followup to Peter Senge's ground-breaking best-seller *The Fifth Discipline*, these essays are grouped in four sections that address all aspects of learning organizations: the guiding ideas behind systems thinking; the theories, methods, and processes for creating a learning organization; the infrastructure of the learning model; and arenas of practice.
ISBN 1-56327-110-9 / 575 pages / $35.00 / Order LEARN-B144

PRODUCTIVITY PRESS, DEPT. BK, P.O. BOX 13390, PORTLAND, OR 97213-0390
Telephone: 1-800-394-6868   Fax: 1-800-394-6286

Feedback Toolkit
16 Tools for Better Communication in the Workplace
Rick Maurer

In companies striving to reduce hierarchy and foster trust and responsible participation, good person-to-person feedback can be as important as sophisticated computer technology in enabling effective teamwork. Feedback is an important map of your situation, a way to tell whether you are "on or off track." Used well, feedback can motivate people to their highest level of performance. Despite its significance, this level of information sharing makes most managers uncomfortable. *Feedback Toolkit* addresses this natural hesitation with an easy-to-grasp 6-step framework and 16 practical and creative approaches for giving and receiving feedback with individuals and groups. Maurer's reality-tested methods in *Feedback Toolkit* are indispensable equipment for managers and teams in every organization.
ISBN 1-56327-056-0 / 109 pages / $12.00 / Order FEED-B144

The Benchmarking Workbook
Adapting Best Practices for Performance Improvement
Gregory H. Watson

Managers today need benchmarking to anticipate trends and maintain competitive advantage. This practical workbook shows you how to do your own benchmarking study. Watson's discussion includes a case study that takes you through each step of the benchmarking process, raises thought-provoking questions, and provides examples of how to use forms for a benchmarking study.
ISBN 1-56327-033-1 / 169 pages / $30.00 / Order BENCHW-B144

Benchmarking Portfolio
Strategic Direction Publishers (ed.)

World Class companies are built on total quality. Get the expertise of over 5 world class consulting groups for less than the cost of commissioning just one report. This portfolio contains 12 executive briefing papers for all of your senior managers, international case studies and practitioner interviews, and a unique benchmarking project organizer. When you're ready to move ahead with Benchmarking, use this portfolio to:
  • Cut Your project preparation time by 75%
  • Wipe out months of unnecessary work
  • Reduce by 50% the cost of running of running a benchmarking project
ISBN 3-908131-07-3 / 4 vols. / 552 pages / $295.00 / Order BENCHF-B144

PRODUCTIVITY PRESS, DEPT. BK, P.O. BOX 13390, PORTLAND, OR 97213-0390
Telephone: 1-800-394-6868   Fax: 1-800-394-6286

Building a Shared Vision
A Leader's Guide to Aligning the Organization
C. Patrick Lewis

This exciting new book presents a step-by-step method for developing your organizational vision. It teaches how to build and maintain a shared vision directed from the top down, but encompassing the views of all the members and stakeholders, and understanding the competitive environment of the organization. Like *Corporate Diagnosis,* this books describes in detail one of the necessary first steps from *Implementing a Lean Management System:* visioning.
ISBN 1-56327-163-X / 150 pages / $45.00 / Order VISION-B144

Building Organizational Fitness
Management Methodology for Transformation and Strategic Advantage
Ryuji Fukuda

The most urgent task for companies today is to take a hard look at the future. To remain competitive, management must nurture a strong capability for self-development and a strong corporate culture, both of which form part of the foundation for improvement. But simply understanding management techniques doesn't mean you know how to use them. You need the tools and technologies for implementation. In *Building Organizational Fitness,* Fukuda extends the power of his managerial engineering methodology into the context of the top management strategic planning role.
ISBN 1-56327-144-3 / 250 pages / $65.00 / Order BFIT-B144

Companywide Audit Pack
Strategic Direction Publishers (ed.)

Any improvement effort first requires a thoughtful assessment of the current state of your organization. This powerful package, compiled from the work of many leaders in the field, is on state of the art company auditing. The portfolio is designed for business managers creating business strategies. Contained in this single comprehensive portfolio are the details of 12 different self-assessment audits. Whether you have done company audits in the past, or now recognize how critical audits are to your strategic plans, this portfolio will provide you with many new and exciting ideas, a deeper understanding, the steps for the audit process, and most importantly, how to use the data you collect to create a powerful and effective company strategy.
ISBN 3-908131-00-6 / 872 pages / $295.00 / Order BMAF-B144

PRODUCTIVITY PRESS, DEPT. BK, P.O. BOX 13390, PORTLAND, OR 97213-0390
Telephone: 1-800-394-6868   Fax: 1-800-394-6286

Cost Reduction Systems
Target Costing and Kaizen Costing
Yasuhiro Monden

Yasuhiro Monden provides a solid framework for implementing two powerful cost reduction systems that have revolutionized Japanese manufacturing management: target costing and kaizen costing. Target costing is a cross-functional system used during the development and design stage for new products. Kaizen costing focuses on cost reduction activities for existing products throughout their life cycles, drawing on approaches such as value analysis. Used together, target costing and kaizen costing form a complete cost reduction system that can be applied from the product's conception to the end of its life cycle. These methods are applicable to both discrete manufacturing and process industries.
ISBN 1-56327-068-4 / 400 pages / $50.00 / Order CRS-B144

Do it Right the Second Time
Benchmarking Best Practices in the Quality Change Process
Peter Merrill

Is your organization looking back on its quality process and saying "it failed"? Are you concerned that TQM is just another fad, only to be replaced by the next improvement movement? Don't jump ship just yet. Everyone experiences failures in their quality improvement process. Successful organizations are different because they learn from their failure: They do it right the second time. In this plain-speaking, easy-to-read book, Peter Merrill helps companies take what they learned from their first attempts at implementing a quality program, rethink the plan, and move forward. He takes you sequentially through the activities required to lead a lasting change from vision to final realization. Each brief chapter covers a specific topic in a framework which leads you directly to the issues that concern your organization.
ISBN 1-56327-175-3 / 225 pages / $27.00 / Order RSEC-B144

Handbook for Personal Productivity
Henry E. Liebling

A little book with a lot of power that will help you become more successful and satisfied at work, as well as in your personal life. This pocket-sized handbook offers sections on personal productivity improvement, team achievement, quality customer service, improving your health, and how to get the most out of workshops and seminars. Special bulk discounts are available (call for more information).
ISBN 1-56327-131-1 / 128 pages / $5.00 paper / Order PERS-B144

PRODUCTIVITY PRESS, DEPT. BK, P.O. BOX 13390, PORTLAND, OR 97213-0390
Telephone: 1-800-394-6868   Fax: 1-800-394-6286

Hoshin Kanri
Policy Deployment for Successful TQM
Yoji Akao (ed.)

Hoshin kanri, the Japanese term for policy deployment, is an approach to strategic planning and quality improvement that has become a pillar of Total Quality Management (TQM) for a growing number of U.S. firms. This book compiles examples of policy deployment that demonstrates how company vision is converted into individual responsibility. It includes practical guidelines, 150 charts and diagrams, and five case studies that illustrate the procedures of hoshin kanri. The six steps to advanced process planning are reviewed and include a five-year vision, one-year plan, deployment to departments, execution, monthly audit, and annual audit.
ISBN 0-915299-57-7 / 241 pages / $65.00 / Order HOSHIN-B144

The Improvement Engine
Creativity and Innovation Through Employee Involvement—
The Kaizen Teian System
JHRA (ed.)

The Improvement Engine offers the most all inclusive information available today on this proven method for increasing employee involvement. Kaizen Teian is a technique developed in Japan for encouraging employees to constantly look for and make improvement suggestions. This book explores the subtleties between designing a moderately successful program and a highly successful one and includes a host of tools, techniques, and case studies.
ISBN 1-56327-010-2 / 195 pages / $40.00 / Order IMPENG-B144

Kaizen Teian 2
Guiding Continuous Improvement Through Employee Suggestions
Japan Human Relations Association (ed.)

Building on the concepts covered in *Kaizen Teian I,* this second volume examines in depth how to implement kaizen teian–a continuous improvement suggestions system. Managers will learn techniques for getting employees to think creatively about workplace improvements and how to run a successful proposal program.
ISBN 0-915299-53-4 / 221 pages (paperback) / $30.00 / Order KT2P-B144

PRODUCTIVITY PRESS, DEPT. BK, P.O. BOX 13390, PORTLAND, OR 97213-0390
Telephone: 1-800-394-6868   Fax: 1-800-394-6286

Making the Numbers Count
The Management Accountant as Change Agent on the World Class Team
Brian H. Maskell

Traditional accounting systems hold back improvement strategies and process innovation. Maskell's timely book addresses the growing phenomenon confronting managers in continuous improvement environments. It unmasks the shortcomings of the management accountant's traditional role and shows the inadequacy of running a business based on financial reports. According to Maskell, in a world class organization, the management accountant can and should take the lead in establishing performance measures that make a difference. Empowering frontline workers and middle managers to effectively improve their operations is one way to do it
ISBN: 1-56327-070-6 / 150 pages, illustrations / $29.00 / Order MNC-B144

Management for Quality Improvement
The 7 New QC Tools
Shigeru Mizuno, ed.

Building on the traditional seven QC tools, these tools were developed specifically for managers. They help in planning, troubleshooting, and communicating with maximum effectiveness at every stage of a quality improvement program. The tools presented in this book represent the most important advance in quality deployment and project management in recent years, and will help you expand the scope of quality efforts companywide.
ISBN 0-915299-29-1 / 323 pages / $65.00 / Order 7QC-B144

Managerial Engineering
Techniques for Improving Quality and Productivity in the Workplace
Ryuji Fukuda

A proven path to managerial success, based on reliable methods developed by one of Japan's leading productivity experts and winner of the coveted Deming Prize for quality. Dr. W. Edwards Deming, world-famous consultant on quality, said that the book "provides an excellent and clear description of the devotion and methods of Japanese management to continual improvement of quality." This book lays the foundations for your most powerful and effective quality improvement efforts. Specific methods covered in the book include CEDAC (the Cause-and-Effect Diagram with the Addition of Cards), IE improvements, small group activities, and stockless production techniques. (Training programs on CEDAC, the award-winning system outlined in this book, are also available from Productivity.)
ISBN 0-915299-09-7 / 208 pages / $45.00 / Order ME-B144

PRODUCTIVITY PRESS, DEPT. BK, P.O. BOX 13390, PORTLAND, OR 97213-0390
Telephone: 1-800-394-6868   Fax: 1-800-394-6286

Performance Measurement for World Class Manufacturing
A Model for American Companies
Brian H. Maskell

If your company is adopting world class manufacturing techniques, you'll need new methods of performance measurement to control production variables. In practical terms, this book describes the new methods of performance measurement and how they are used in a changing environment. For manufacturing managers as well as cost accountants, it provides a theoretical foundation of these innovative methods supported by extensive practical examples. The book specifically addresses performance measures for delivery, process time, production flexibility, quality, and finance.
ISBN 0-915299-99-2 / 429 pages / $55.00 / Order PERFM-B144

Putting Performance Measurement to Work
Building Focus and Sustaining Improvement
(Action Learning software application)
Learner First with Brian H. Maskell

For optimal results in your improvement efforts, the introduction of new performance measures needs to go hand in hand with the introduction of new manufacturing techniques. You choose what area of improvement to focus on, determine the improvement, determine the measures, and put them in place. Then you move to the next area to be improved and you do the same thing. Easy, right? This software application will teach you, coach you, help you determine then achieve your goals and lead you to success.
ISBN 1-56327-171-0 /Manual 250 pages / $495.00 / Order PERFSW-B144

Secrets of a Successful Employee Recognition System
Daniel C. Boyle

As the human resource manager of a failing manufacturing plant, Dan Boyle was desperate to find a way to motivate employees and break down the barrier between management and the union. He came up with a simple idea to say thank you to your employees for doing their job. In *Secrets to a Successful Employee Recognition System,* Boyle outlines how to begin and run a 100 Club program. Filled with case studies and detailed guidelines, this book underscores the power behind thanking your employees for a job well done.
ISBN 1-56327-083-8 / 250 pages / $25.00 / Order SECRET-B144

Productivity Press, Dept. BK, P.O. Box 13390, Portland, OR 97213-0390
Telephone: 1-800-394-6868   Fax: 1-800-394-6286

Thoughtware
Change the Thinking and the Organization Will Change Itself
J. Philip Kirby and D.H. Hughes

In order to facilitate true change in an organization, its thinking patterns need to be the first thing to change. Your employees need more than empowerment. They need to move from doing their jobs to doing whatever is needed for the good of the entire organization. Thoughtware is the underlying platform on which every organization operates, the set of assumptions upon which the organization is structured. When you understand and change thoughtware, the tools and techniques of continuous improvement become incredibly powerful.

ISBN 1-56327-106-0 / 200 pages / $35.00 / Order THOUG-B144

Stepping Up to ISO 14000
Integrating Environmental Quality with ISO 9000 and TQM
Subhash C. Puri

The newest ISO standards, announced in mid-1996, require environmentally-friendly practices in every aspect of a manufacturing business, from factory design and raw material acquisition to the production, packaging, distribution, and ultimate disposal of the product. Here's a comprehensible overview and implementation guide to the standards that's also the only one to show how they fit with current ISO 9000 efforts and other companywide programs for Total Quality Management (TQM).

ISBN 1-56327-129-X / 280 pages / $39.00 / Order STPISO-B144

TO ORDER: Write, phone, or fax Productivity Press, Dept. BK, P.O. Box 13390, Portland, OR 97213-0390, phone 1-800-394-6868, fax 1-800-394-6286. Send check or charge to your credit card (American Express, Visa, MasterCard accepted).

U.S. ORDERS: Add $5 shipping for first book, $2 each additional for UPS surface delivery. Add $5 for each AV program containing 1 or 2 tapes; add $12 for each AV program containing 3 or more tapes. We offer attractive quantity discounts for bulk purchases of individual titles; call for more information.

ORDER BY E-MAIL: Order 24 hours a day from anywhere in the world. Use either address:
To order: service@ppress.com
To view the online catalog and/or order: http://www.ppress.com

Productivity Press, Dept. BK, P.O. Box 13390, Portland, OR 97213-0390
Telephone: 1-800-394-6868   Fax: 1-800-394-6286

QUANTITY DISCOUNTS: For information on quantity discounts, please contact our sales department.

INTERNATIONAL ORDERS: Write, phone, or fax for quote and indicate shipping method desired. For international callers, telephone number is 503-235-0600 and fax number is 503-235-0909. Prepayment in U.S. dollars must accompany your order (checks must be drawn on U.S. banks). When quote is returned with payment, your order will be shipped promptly by the method requested.

NOTE: Prices are in U.S. dollars and are subject to change without notice.

Continue Your Learning with In-House Training and Consulting from the Productivity Consulting Group

Consulting Services

For over a decade, an expansive client base continues to recommend the Productivity Consulting Group (PCG) to colleagues eager to accelerate their improvement efforts. We have established a lasting improvement process with companies from various industries, including textiles, printing and packaging, chemicals, and heavy equipment.

Assignments vary from results-driven trainings on the tools of Lean Production, to broad total company conversion projects dealing with strategic intent through organization design/ redesign. Tailoring our methodology to accommodate site-specific organizational and performance considerations is a real strength of the Productivity Consulting Group.

Educational Resources

Our products and services are leading-edge, and have been used by most every company in the Fortune 500 and beyond. Topics include: Quick Changeover, Visual Workplace, Lean Production Systems, Total Productive Maintenance, and Mistake-Proofing.

We offer the following opportunities to enhance your improvement efforts: National Conferences, Training Events, Plant Tours, Industrial Study Missions, Master Series Workshops, and Newsletters.

Call the Productivity Consulting Group and learn how we can provide consulting services and educational resources customized to fit your changing needs.

Telephone: 1-800-966-5423 (U.S. only) or 1-203-846-3777
Fax: 1-203-846-6883